The Economics of Networks and Digital Platforms

The Economics of Networks and Digital Platforms

Henrique Schneider

BEP

BUSINESS EXPERT PRESS

Leader in applied, concise business books

The Economics of Networks and Digital Platforms

First published in 2025 by
Business Expert Press, LLC
222 East 46th Street, New York, NY 10017
www.businessexpertpress.com

ISBN-13: 978-1-63742-768-2 (paperback)
ISBN-13: 978-1-63742-769-9 (e-book)

Business Expert Press Economics and Public Policy Collection

First edition: 2025

10 9 8 7 6 5 4 3 2 1

Description

Step into the future of business with this essential guide to the digital economy, where network effects and data-driven strategies are rewriting the rules of success for industry leaders.

This textbook comprehensively explores network economics, focusing on **digital platforms** and **ecosystems**. It delves into the fundamental principles of network effects, where the value of a service increases as more people use it and examines various pricing models essential in network-based businesses. Governance is another critical aspect, emphasizing the importance of establishing trust and reliable management practices within digital platforms. By the end of this book, you will feel confident in your understanding of these complex topics.

The book highlights the pivotal role of **data** in the network economy and keeps you abreast of the latest trends in the network and platform economy. It showcases how these trends, such as the increasing influence of data and network effects, are shaping the future and significantly influencing the present landscape. Key examples include industry giants like Google, Amazon, Facebook, Uber, and Airbnb, which are at the forefront of **leveraging network effects** and data to dominate their respective markets. This book lets you feel informed and ready to navigate these trends.

Designed for **students** and **professionals** alike, this textbook combines theoretical foundations with practical insights, making it a valuable resource for **understanding the dynamic world of digital platforms**. Whether you are studying economics, business, or technology, this book provides the knowledge and tools needed to navigate and succeed in the evolving digital economy.

Contents

Preface

This textbook introduces the economics of networks and digital platforms. It deals with network effects, pricing models in networks, governance for building trust, and the importance of data. Integrating insights from economics and management, two related questions will be answered:

- How can network and digital platforms be designed to work as business models?
- How does the economic machine room of these business models work?

The first question is important for managers and practitioners responsible for business models' operations and outcomes. The second question addresses a long-standing research program in economics. Answering these two questions and, consequently, tying in management and economics create synergies that lead to new, more profound insights and better, more successful practices.

Digital business models are on the rise. They seem to be more than just paving the way to the future—they seem to be conquering the present. Google, Amazon, Facebook, Uber, Airbnb, WeChat, and Alibaba represent just a few examples of such businesses. What unifies them, however, is that they are digital, especially their design as networks, platforms, or ecosystems. This type of business model—that is, with such a design—relies on network effects.

Network effects occur when the increase of users or a network, platform, or ecosystem benefits those incoming users, the remaining users, and the entire network, platform, and ecosystem. This is easier said than done. While economics has long focused on how these effects work, it has generally neglected how to create them. While managers usually focus on creating network effects, they forget that these effects result from specific choices in the governance of a network, platform, or ecosystem.

This textbook explains how this fits together and how the economics of networks and digital platforms go well beyond network effects. It combines economics and managerial studies to analyze and configure networks, platforms, and ecosystems. It draws on a mix of quantitative and qualitative elements. It includes a particularly large number of examples, including even some from the non-digital environment, to clarify the value added by digitization. The objective of the learning experience in this book is to identify and understand what networks are and how they work. This, in turn, can be applied to different examples of digital business models.

This textbook suits introductory and specialized courses focusing on network or platform economics. It is also designed for digitization, digital business models, or business model development syllabi. It can be used in business administration and economics courses and degree programs. This textbook is also suitable as a supplement for business informatics, applied computer science, and business psychology. It can be used to support courses teaching the basics of networks from the information technology perspective or to support teaching units examining the behavior of economic actors. Finally, this book is designed for practitioners who wish to gain more insights. Ultimately, it is a practical business book with a solid theoretical foundation.

This textbook is broken down into four chapters:

Chapter 1 gives a general overview of the topic of this book, establishing how the discussion about networks and platforms relates to several other issues in contemporary economics and business. This chapter builds the basic network and platform economics vocabulary and discusses foundational topics such as the business model and digitization. The chapter introduces the core ideas of network and platform business models, which will be expanded in the following chapter.

Chapter 2 is about network effects and explores the different types of these effects. Paying attention to the difference between mere effects of scale and full-blown network effects, this chapter delves into mechanisms for igniting and maintaining the beneficial mechanics and results of networks, platforms, and ecosystems. It also discusses the *hen or egg* problem, a practical conundrum concerning which was first the network or its effects.

Chapter 3 addresses network pricing models, especially in digital networks and platforms. It develops qualitative and quantitative approaches to pricing; discusses price differentiation, service levels, and lock-ins; and ends with the hard questions regarding practical decisions on pricing.

Chapter 4 analyses the governance structures of networks and platforms. These structures are based on trust, which must be continuously cultivated to grow and become more cohesive. The chapter analyses instruments deployed in networks and platforms to manage trust. It concludes with a general discussion centered on the future of the network and platform economy, identifying several research priorities that will be particularly important.

All chapters are prepared didactically. Each chapter:

- is introduced with a learning agenda;
- is concluded with a summary and outlook;
- contains a critical reflection on its content;
- features 30 questions or tasks designed as round-ups of its contents: 10 questions focusing on consolidating the content, 10 on applying core ideas in practical setups, and 10 on transferring these ideas to more intricate cases.
- finally, each chapter includes an annotated bibliography with additional literature.

Various supplementary elements, such as examples, background information, or thought experiments, are integrated into the text. A glossary is provided at the end of the book.

Embarking on the journey through this textbook, you will gain theoretical knowledge and practical skills essential in today's digital economy. Whether you are a student eager to understand the complexities of network and platform economics, a professional aiming to enhance your business acumen, or a researcher seeking to delve deeper into this evolving field, this book will serve as your comprehensive guide. Integrating insights from economics and management offers a unique perspective that bridges the gap between theory and practice. As you explore the intricacies of digital business models, network effects, pricing strategies, and governance structures, you will be equipped with the tools to innovate and lead in the digital age. This textbook is more than an academic resource; it catalyzes your success in navigating and mastering the dynamics of digital platforms and ecosystems. Dive in, and let the knowledge and insights within propel you toward achieving excellence and significantly impacting the digital business world.

CHAPTER 1

The Big Picture

Learning Agenda

This chapter provides a general overview of networks, digital platforms, and ecosystems. It introduces the technical terms involved and distinguishes between business models based on networks and pipelines. Once you have read this chapter, you will be familiar with digital business models, especially digital networks, platforms, and ecosystems. This chapter is organized into 10 sections. After going through them, you will be able to:

- Section 1.1: categorize the significance of networks and platforms in the economy.
- Section 1.2: differentiate terminologically between networks, platforms, and ecosystems.
- Section 1.3: define transaction costs.
- Section 1.4: recognize the importance of investments, capital expenditures, and operational expenditures.
- Section 1.5: reflect the contents of a business model.
- Section 1.6: differentiate between a pipeline and a network business model.
- Section 1.7: typify network business models.
- Section 1.8: analyze the potential economic implications of network business models.
- Section 1.9: gain an overview of the controversies associated with platforms.
- Section 1.10: critically reflect the contents of this chapter.

1.1 Network Economics: An Old Unknown

Uber, the world's largest taxi-style service provider, owns no cars. Facebook, the world's largest provider of media services, does not produce any content. Alibaba, the world's largest retailer, has no warehouse. Airbnb, the world's largest accommodation provider, does not own a building.

But let us start somewhere else. Let us examine the biggest companies in the world and how the top 10 companies have changed: Industrial companies still led the ranking of the largest companies by market capitalization in 2008 (Forbes 2021). PetroChina took first place, followed by Exxon and General Electric. The first service provider, the Chinese bank ICBC, came in fifth place. Microsoft came in seventh place. Yet, at the time, Microsoft did not rely on a network or platform business model. The largest company at the time with a business model based on network economics was AT&T. It ranked 10th.

Wait! Microsoft was not a platform, but AT&T was; how is this possible? At first glance, it would seem counterintuitive. At the time, Microsoft focused on producing software and selling it to single customers. This type of business model is best described as a pipeline, which will be reviewed later in this chapter. By contrast, AT&T was enabling people to interact with each other. Customers use the telephone network to reach each other. AT&T, with its network and services, facilitates the exchange. This is a platform or network business model.

The ranking of the world's largest companies looks very different in 2024, not even two decades later. Microsoft, following a platform business model with its cloud since 2010, ranks first. Apple, which subscribed early on to networks and ecosystems thinking, comes second. Nvidia, a hybrid between pipeline and network, stands in third with Google's Alphabet in fourth and Amazon in fifth place. The first half of the top 10 all pursue network economics in their business models. The list is completed by pipelines: TSMC, the producer of semiconductors, Berkshire Hathaway, the investment company, and the pharmaceutical Eli Lilly (Forbes 2024).

Six out of 10 of the companies with the highest market capitalization are platforms, and all five of the top five pursue network economics. Yes, rankings are problematic, but they indicate what is happening in the economy. Platform business models are here to stay, and they are changing the way companies and customers interact. Their success can be read in the ranking, or rather, in the changes in ranking. Of course, the companies sponsoring platforms and networks in this ranking pursue digital business models. The network economy and digital business models have become virtually synonymous. We tend to forget, however, that network business models are, in fact, age-old and have not always been digital, let alone worth billions of dollars. Examples of more traditional network business models include:

- private television stations;
- telephone services;
- network marketing or multilevel marketing;
- bazaars such as the Al-Madina Souq in Aleppo or the Kapalı Çarşı, the big bazaar, in Istanbul;
- marketplaces such as the weekly farmers' market or the Chinese night and animal markets;
- fairs and exhibitions;
- *Friendly Societies* in the British Isles and *Auxiliary Societies* in the United States.

    These examples show that networks have a long history of being the foundation for business models. But if Alibaba (the digital platform) and the vegetable market in Vila Mariana (a neighborhood in São Paulo, Brazil) share common features, what exactly is a network? Which features do all networks share? What is network economics?

A *network* refers to the reciprocal interaction of different people who transact using a common infrastructure or interaction structure.

In the *network economy*, the participants utilize this interaction structure to achieve economic goals.

A *network business model* entails developing and maintaining the common infrastructure or interaction structure. The network's sponsor facilitates the interactions between participants in this common infrastructure or interaction structure, capitalizing on the connections realized there.

In this book, the terms *network* and *platform* are used synonymously to simplify the text. Some nuance will be introduced later. There is a slight difference between these terms and ecosystem, which will be introduced later.

These definitions cover various elements. They will be explored in greater depth throughout this textbook. The centerpiece of the network—any network—is the common infrastructure or interaction structure. This concept implies several things:

- It involves the connections between people linked in a network.
- These numerous connections, their intensity, and the number of people participating in them are constantly in flux.
- These connections have an open relationship with each other; for example, they can be aligned in the same direction, in opposite directions, or independent of each other.
- One person may have any number of connections of varying intensity to the others.
- Conversely, a number of other people may have a direct or indirect connection of varying intensity with one person.
- The specific people who have connections to each other can change.
- The network has no objective other than facilitating connections of type $n{:}n$, that is, any number of people to any number of people.

The concept of the interaction structure does not originate in economic theory. Like the network concept, it stems from another social science, anthropology. Even if borrowed, the term does not mean precisely the same in both disciplines. Social networks, as envisioned by anthropology, arise culturally. The network economy tends to have one or more people who facilitate or control the interaction structure. Networks, according to anthropology, do not have a sponsor. Their governance is customs, beliefs, and culture. In economics and management, network business models are sponsored by an economic agent. This agent, a company, steers the network actively. Platform business models are controlled by a company, the sponsor of the network.

The souq requires several people to assign the individual trading places and to keep order. Friendly Societies and other associations require committees to prepare programs and organize events. A telephone network requires an operating company that sets up the services and guarantees the connections. Digital networks also rely on a company to program the site, create interfaces, or invest money in marketing. The control function of a network—later, we will see that this function is better named *governance*—includes managing four central connection types—they are known as the *four C's*:

1. creation: setting up, or programming, an intermediation structure, the software, algorithm, or app;
2. curation: setting up and enforcing the rules of the network;
3. customization: engineering the benefits for the users of the network;
4. consumption: steering users of the network to interact via the network.

The company sponsoring the platform exerts control over it by steering the users to turn potential connections into specific interactions on the platform. The more successful the sponsor is in this conversion, the larger the benefits for the users and for the sponsor.

1.2 Network, Platform, Ecosystem

As mentioned above, the terminology can be tricky. There is no standard vocabulary yet. For this reason, it is better to set the terms used here straight. A *network* refers to the reciprocal interaction of different people transacting via a common infrastructure or interaction structure. *Network* and *platform* are synonyms. A *digital platform* is a *digital network* is a digital business model. As such, a company sponsors the platform or network. The sponsor develops or arranges for the core of the necessary programming, that is, the algorithm, software, or app, and sets up the platform's governance to exert control over it, following the four C's. To bring in some nuance, an *ecosystem* is a controlled link between several interaction structures based on a digital network but promoting additional subnetworks. In other words, an ecosystem is a platform for platforms or a network of networks. The ecosystem, too, has a sponsor if it is a business model.

Economic theory uses a different term for the platform or network: *multisided business model*. Technically, it is an exact term. It says a business model consists of an intermediary connecting two or more sides. The sides are the groups of people using the platform. For example, people making a payment are one group or side. People receiving the payment are the other group or side. PayPal intermediates between these two sides, facilitating the payment, or flow of money, between them. PayPal connects the two sides and is called a two-sided business model. Now, could PayPal collect all transaction data and sell it to another agent, such as a data aggregator? Then, it would be servicing a third side. In this case, it would be a three-sided business model. This ability to adapt the general definition to specific connections of a platform is the elegance of the technical term multisided business model.

For clarification, these definitions speak of people or agents, including both natural people and companies. The term *person* is a good choice since it is neutral about the person. Anyone who can act can be a person. The term person attributes will and intentions to the agent. That is what economics is all about: people acting and reflecting their actions and plans. Therefore, person and agent will be used synonymously, referring to anyone, including companies.

Many other terms are associated with the network economy in addition to the ones reviewed so far. This is not the place for discussing and differentiating them all. In the end, there will (probably) never be a common denominator for all the terms. And that is no bad thing.

After all, the important thing is how digital platforms, networks, and ecosystems work—not how the terminology is set up.

One distinction is important, however. Some properties, such as the network effect (see below), apply to all networks. They are at work in the Canadian cattle auction and the South Korean e-commerce platform G-Market; they are the core logic of the PDF standard for file sharing and Google's search engine. However, some properties only hold to digital platforms or networks. In this book, when we speak generally of platform, network, or ecosystem, we discuss general properties applying to all types, including non-digital. Referring to specific properties of digital networks will always be marked by the word digital.

The importance of this differentiation goes hand in hand with a crucial question for economists and managers: If it is the case that networks have existed for a long time, why have they only burst onto the scene with full force in the last 10 years? Why is it that economic success is only now being associated with network business models? Why do younger people with an entrepreneurial spirit dream of finding a place on platforms and in ecosystems instead of starting everything from scratch? The answer is *transaction costs*. The more digital networks lower transaction costs, the more successful they are.

1.3 Transaction Costs

The American economist Michael Munger frequently shares an anecdote from his oral doctoral examination. His mentor at the time, Douglass North, who later won the Nobel Prize, asked him why getting everyone working in a company on the same level of information was so difficult. Munger then proceeded to draw a mathematical model on the board, and North interrupted him just as he was about to draw a second derivation. Just as you would talk to a child, North is said to have said to the examinee: "Mike, it's the transaction costs."

Transaction costs play a crucial role in economic theory. They cover all costs that arise in connection with a business transaction. This means they are not incurred in producing goods but in transferring goods from one economic subject to another. Munger (2018) gives the following examples of transaction costs:

- initiation costs, for example, making contact;
- information procurement costs, for example, finding a contractual partner, obtaining references, or checking reputation;
- agreement costs, for example, formulating a contract;
- handling costs, for example, transport costs, fees for intermediaries;
- change costs/adjustment costs, for example, changes to deadlines, quality, quantity, and price;
- control costs, for example, monitoring compliance with deadlines, quality, quantity, price, and confidentiality agreements.

Transaction costs do not always occur as cash outflows, of course. Frequently, they occur as costs in the sense of time spent or risks assumed. The concept of costs in economic theory is an open one. It encompasses all actions people must undertake before entering into a transaction with another person. Often, transaction costs keep people from interacting altogether.

Here lies the beauty of networks. Networks lower transaction costs. They are particularly powerful when the transaction costs of a market are high because they diminish this cost.

Think of a company trying to enter a new market. There is so much information to digest, people to get to know, and contracts to set up. These are examples of transaction costs. A specifically high transaction cost involves establishing contacts in the target market. The firm would need to do a lot of one-to-one presentations, but not all of them are successful. The firm will have to talk to local partners. But not all of them are good. The firm will have to apply for a lot of permits. But it does not know which are necessary. The network helps. For example, the firm can lower these transaction costs by joining an association of companies in the target market. That association will establish links to other companies. Instead of getting to know partners serially, the firm joins a pool of partners. This lowers the transaction cost of screening the market for partnerships. Let us think this through:

The Charm of Associations

When a German company in Germany seeks a business relationship in Mexico, it is confronted with high transaction costs, such as not knowing anyone in Mexico, not knowing the culture, facing language barriers, and much more. One way of lowering these costs is to join a German Mexican Chamber of Commerce.

While this does not automatically lead to finding a partner, the Chamber of Commerce has a directory of members listing various Mexican companies. Furthermore, not every company can afford to join the Chamber of Commerce. As a result, there is also a certain degree of quality control when selecting a membership. Only those willing and able to pay, that is, it stands to reason that only relatively more successful companies allocate money to join. Finally, there is the element of peer pressure and control. The companies in the Chamber are not anonymous. They care about their image vis-à-vis the other members. Finally, if it is not possible for the company to find a suitable business partner, it can still use the Chamber of Commerce as an intermediary.

But the German company will have to pay to join the Chamber. It faces a trade-off: doing everything, which is transaction cost-intensive, or joining the Chamber, which comes at the cost of membership. The higher the transaction cost, the relatively cheaper joining the network appears.

It would have been a different scenario if this German company had already been active in Mexico and collaborated with many partner companies. If this were the case, the company would probably have found a new partner in Mexico without joining the Chamber of Commerce. If the German company already has experience in Mexico, its transaction costs are lower. Transaction costs are, therefore, relative to the specific situation of the actor.

The example shows how transaction costs are often the reason non-digital networks exist. They are, in fact, a way of reducing such transaction costs. Yet, in a market with no or only minimal transaction costs, networks will not be able to establish or maintain themselves. This is because networks themselves generate transaction costs.

Illustrating this point: Trade fairs, or exhibitions, are platforms. There is a sponsor, the company organizing the fair, and there are users, the businesses using the fair to showcase their products, and the people participating usually looking for products and partners. Fairs are increasingly facing challenges, and the number of exhibitors and visitors is shrinking. The reason is that costs and transaction costs are associated with using the fair. One must buy space, build a stand, or pay the staff. Visitors dedicate time and sometimes pay an entrance fee. There are ways to lower these costs, especially using the internet. In other words, fairs did a good job of lowering transaction costs in a pre-digital world. However, as the digital environment takes over, fairs become too costly in the face of the digital alternative. Again, the point is that the trade-off between costs and transaction costs is always relative.

The improvement in information technology and the spread of the internet have significantly reduced transaction costs. This has two effects: First, it makes certain markets and many non-digital networks less attractive, and second, it makes networks that can leverage this reduction in transaction costs more attractive. These are the digital platforms and ecosystems.

The example of online platforms substituting trade fairs is just one of many ways networks replace networks. Other examples are:

- Those looking to sell their old hairdryer used to have to spend a lot of time finding a buyer. You had to go from second-hand shop to second-hand shop and offer the old appliance there. At some point, people just disposed of it because they perceived it as not worth soliciting an unlimited number of shops. In other words, the transaction costs swallowed up the value of the old appliance. Then eBay came along, and the transaction costs were reduced to the few minutes it took to create a profile and place a listing. At the same time, many more people could become aware of the intention to sell. Lower transaction costs and greater reach from intermediation make eBay, a network business model, more attractive than a second-hand shop, another network business model.

- An advert in a printed daily newspaper could only reach a limited amount of people, depending on its circulation. The digitization of newspapers meant that an advertisement could reach many more people than the number of copies printed. As a result, placing the ad in the digital paper became more attractive because of the enhanced reach. The personalization of most websites also ensures a more precise target public. This means that the transaction costs from dispersion losses are reduced. Again, lower transaction costs and greater reach make the online newspaper, a network business model, much more attractive than a printed newspaper, another network business model.

These examples illustrate that networks can compete. Yet networks, especially digital networks of today, compete with pipeline business models through lower transaction costs: Uber has lower transaction costs than taxis, Airbnb has lower transaction costs than hotels, and Zalando has lower transaction costs than fashion outlets.

This calls for an important question: How do network business models make money? Lowering transaction costs for users is the reason the network is popular with users, but it does not automatically entail any reward for the sponsor. This reward must be extracted from users. But first, the cost structure of the network business model, especially in its digital form, needs some explanation.

1.4 Investment, CAPEX, OPEX

Networks, digital platforms, and ecosystems build connections. They aim to create real, specific interactions or exchange relationships from the number of possible connections. The successful implementation of this interaction is called *intermediation*.

The network sponsor makes certain advance payments to create an environment that leads to intermediation. These advance payments are called investments. Investment refers to the long-term commitment of financial resources in material or nonmaterial assets to utilize these assets and generate a profit. An investment in this respect may take various forms, such as the purchase of a machine or the development of a program, the investment of money on a stock exchange, or the development of a brand.

Investments lead to high cash outflows in the present and possible cash inflows in the future. The extent of these inflows and whether they can offset the cash outflow constitute the risk of every investment.

On that basis, economic theory further differentiates between:

- Capital expenditures (CAPEX) comprise a company's longer-term investments. CAPEX aim to increase production and productivity and generate or increase sales and profits. In non-digital networks, this includes building infrastructure such as telephone lines, railway tracks, and so on. In the case of digital platforms and ecosystems, this includes programming or establishing a brand.
- Operational Expenditures (OPEX) comprise all expenditures necessary to guarantee a functioning business. In the case of non-digital networks, this includes personnel and operating resources. In the case of digital platforms and ecosystems, this includes personnel and electrical energy.

This differentiation has palpable consequences: Investments and, therefore, CAPEX are necessary for establishing the network. They are not part of the costs since the value of the investment remains intact over the long term. (Actually, that is more theory than practice, but it is the theory used here. In practice, if companies fail, the investment is lost; if the company succeeds, the investment may be recuperated at a premium. But let's go back to the theory:) For instance, many companies spend considerable money to build a brand. These expenditures are investments since the brand's built-up value remains intact. The notion is that the expenditure remains within the company as a value—as the brand's value. The more recognized the brand, the more valuable the network. Investments and, consequently, CAPEX increase capitalization. They need not be compensated for by the specific good or service price since they are a valuable asset in the company's balance.

The good or service offered by the platform's sponsor is intermediation. What price must users of these intermediation services pay? In principle, they only need to pay for OPEX, which will be revised later in Chapter 3.

To give an example of a non-digital network business, there are brokers for diamonds. They intermediate between buyers and sellers. Their assets are their reputation and contacts. Building them up takes time and dedication. This is their investment or CAPEX. But no matter how much of either they have, they will need compensation for their operating expenses for the intermediation to work. For example, they need to fly between Delhi and Johannesburg, contact people, use time to tap their networks, and incur costs associated with setting up deals. These are OPEX. They will charge at least OPEX (and a margin for CAPEX) for intermediating.

OPEX is reduced with information technology and the internet. A digital platform does not need to fly between Delhi and Johannesburg. It also takes hardly any time to select contacts. Regarding digital platforms, OPEX is generally fixed costs, such as rent, staff, and energy. It is irrelevant to the total amount of OPEX whether the platform can realize one or billions of interactions. The individual intermediation has no or only a minor influence on the level of OPEX. Since the OPEX per intermediation, or better, per intermediated transaction, is (virtually) zero in digital platforms, the platform can offer the intermediation at no cost.

Let us nuance this last sentence: Since the digital platform has almost no OPEX per intermediated transaction, it *could* offer its services for free. However, the platform wants to price at least some of its services. First, it wants to recuperate at least some of its capital expenses. Second, it wants to turn a profit. Most digital platforms are at ease with offering some, even all, intermediations for free. It makes so much money with some of its services that it can offer the others at zero price. Or, since it offers many intermediations for free, it can cash in on some other transactions. This seems counterintuitive. It is—and it will be further explored later when we review pricing strategies.

Digital networks reduce transaction costs and OPEX, which is a double success factor compared to pipeline business models and non-digital networks. This also means that digital networks can scale up their operations by increasing their reach. On the other hand, they require high investments and, consequently, CAPEX.

Expenses and costs are only one, albeit an important, aspect of a platform's whole business. And that is what platforms are: A network business model is, first and foremost, a business model. As such, it has an inner logic and structure, as do business models. This leads to the question of how business models are set up.

1.5 Business Model

Business activity involves having ideas, acting on them, and dealing with the consequences. Having an idea is, in and by itself, a risky undertaking. Maybe the idea is already there, and maybe no one finds it interesting. Acting on the idea bears even more risk. If risk materializes, one must deal with it. Usually, there are four types of risk associated with business activity:

1. Innovation risk is associated with the business idea. The target group may not receive it well and turn the business model into a flop, but it might also be very well received and become a huge success.

2. The implementation risk is associated with the entrepreneur's operational activities: They may not have sufficient discipline, knowledge, abilities, and other similar qualities to follow up on the idea. They may also be a strong manager who can implement the business idea within a structured framework.

3. Time risk involves the time lag between the timing of decisions, their implementation, and the possible repercussions. The company is established at a certain point, yet it has a future

point as a frame of reference; earnings are only realized in the future, and costs are incurred along the way.

4. Information risk concerns the entrepreneur's lack of information regarding their business model. First, they are unaware of the potential market; second, the market is constantly changing.

These are all risks that entrepreneurs bear. They cannot—and should not—be eliminated since the function of companies is to assume risks. Entrepreneurial activity is thus a calculated bet. It is calculated because the entrepreneur can assess the risks to some degree. It is a bet because entrepreneurs cannot know whether their idea will offset all risks. The bet pays off if returns compensate for the risks, something that can only materialize in the future.

Despite this, business administration has developed techniques for addressing such risks. Better: to make business ideas, implementation, and associated risks systematic. The most important such technique is the business model. This chapter has already mentioned it many times.

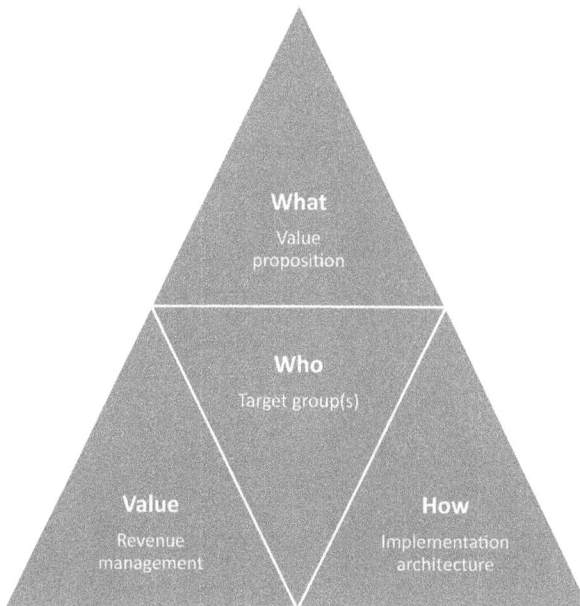

Figure 1.1 Business model (own illustration based on Gassmann et al. 2020)

It will now be explored in more depth. The business model systematizes and summarizes what is most important regarding entrepreneurial activity: Who are the target customer groups? What is being promised to customers? How is the promise fulfilled? How does the promise translate into revenue?

A *business model* is a plan for implementing an entrepreneurial idea that is individual to the company and subjective. The business model systematizes the most important entrepreneurial decisions on implementing the idea and handling risks. It has four dimensions (Figure 1.1; Gassmann et al. 2020):

- Target group(s): Who are the customers or customer groups, what do they expect and value, and how does our business idea benefit them?
- Value proposition: What is the value proposition for customers, what do we promise them, and what makes us unique in their eyes?
- Implementation architecture: How is the value proposition implemented to ensure the promises are kept? Which infrastructure, processes, and people do we need? How is the customer journey?
- Revenue mechanisms: How does the fulfillment of the value proposition generate revenue? How is capital raised and managed?

Let us go through the different parts of the business model using Uber as an example. Its original business idea was to connect surplus individual mobility capacity (i.e., free car seats) with people willing to travel. The business model tells us the inner logic of Uber's business idea (following Schneider 2017):

The target groups are the customers or customer groups that the business model aims to reach. Customers or customer groups are people who can benefit from the implementation of the business model's idea. They value their benefit from the business idea, so they are willing to offer economic compensation to the business owner. Regarding network business models, a major benefit is that different target groups are connected. Uber has two target groups. The first are people with surplus individual mobility capacity and are prepared to convert this surplus into income. The second is people who want convenient, personalized, and flexible mobility solutions.

The value proposition describes the benefits promised to the target groups. Benefits include all aspects that improve the lives of those in the target groups. Benefits are the reason for target groups to turn into customers. A business's value proposition can involve products, services, or experiences. What constitutes a value proposition and a benefit in the eyes of the target group is multifaceted and subjective. It is up to the business model to figure out which value proposition best suits the target groups. In Uber's business model, there is a value proposition for the first target group: to convert surplus mobility capacity, that is, an empty car seat, into income. The second target group's value proposition is to get a car ride at any time using a simple matching algorithm, the app.

The implementation architecture specifies how promises are kept to the target groups. Value propositions are promises. Implementation architecture organizes value creation by structuring processes, activities, resources, capabilities, and partners. Reducing transaction costs is one of the most important aspects of the service architecture in network business models. In Uber's case, simple mobility at a swipe requires a functioning and user-friendly app. Anytime mobility assumes that enough drivers are available at any time. This means it is for the service architecture to build resources and define and control processes to implement these elements. These include programming the app, making the network known, building the brand, and attracting enough people within both target groups. Two aspects are of particular importance here. The brand must be popularized as quickly as possible since the more popular it is, the more people will use the app. Uber has invested virtually all its initial funding in advertising and brand development to achieve this. On the other hand, the app must lower the transaction costs for both target groups. This is why it handles aspects that involve high transaction costs, such as geographical localization, rating, and pricing.

The revenue mechanism explains how the business model becomes capable of generating revenue. This includes two aspects. On the one hand, the capital must be managed. Businesses need capital to invest, liquidity to pursue day-to-day operations, and stability to meet long-term capital commitments. Naturally, businesses need revenue and money inflow from their target groups. The business model generates a profit if the revenues exceed the costs of the service architecture. Regarding capital management, Uber needed capital to set up the algorithm and make itself known. Initially, marketing was a significant investment in creating a vast network. Searching for investors proved to be one of the company's most important challenges in the first 10 years of its existence. Generating revenue for operations is done via the app itself. It has a pricing mechanism. This sets the price that the second target group pays to the first. Uber retains a portion of this price as revenue per intermediation.

1.6 Pipeline and Network

At the beginning of this chapter, two types of business models were mentioned: the pipeline and the network. Let us see the distinction between these types.

Figure 1.2 shows a pipeline business model, frequently called a traditional business model. Here, value is created by the same company step by step, that is, linearly. Figure 1.2 shows such a possible linear value chain. The activities involved in creating value in traditional business models include production planning, procurement, manufacturing, marketing, storage, distribution, and quality control. In a pipeline business model, one company organizes the linear process of adding value. The same company keeps control of all production steps and transactions between them. The company aligns all activities of its parts with the same goal: production or rendering a service. The revenue mechanism of the pipeline business model is to sell a product or render a service, which stands at the end of the chain. Examples of such business models include:

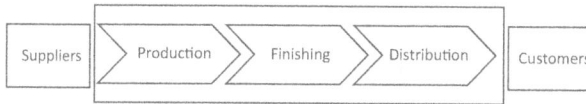

Figure 1.2 Pipeline, the traditional business model (own illustration)

- Traditional production chain: Volkswagen designs and manu-factures cars, for which it establishes its own engineering and construction facilities and sales channels.
- Traditional retail: The neighborhood bakery buys semifinished products and sells baked goods. It does this using its own employees, baking facilities, purchasing, and direct contact with customers.
- Traditional educational programs: Higher education institutions typically employ their buildings and staff to implement an educational concept that has been developed in-house.

Figure 1.3 shows a network business model, a two-sided platform. The network business model connects both sides, Target Groups 1 and 2. The network is organized and controlled by the platform sponsor. This sponsor facilitates access to the network for the target groups and, consequently, the possibility of finding each other in the network. As soon as this possibility becomes real, the platform facilitates an interaction. The interaction develops between the connected target groups. Yet, it is the platform's contribution that brings them together. This service is called intermediation. In the platform business model, the network's sponsor only brings people, or groups of people, together to transact. It neither aligns all their activities with a single goal for all nor does it implement the transactions themselves. It enables transactions.

The revenue mechanism is not specified here. The platform provider seeks to generate revenue with the intermediation. It does not matter whether the individual intermediation is paid for by one or both target groups or whether pure access to the platform is paid for by one or both target groups: There are various conceivable forms of revenue mechanism. They are covered in more detail later in this book.

Figure 1.3 shows a platform comprising two target groups, a so-called two-sided market. The ability of the platform to add and

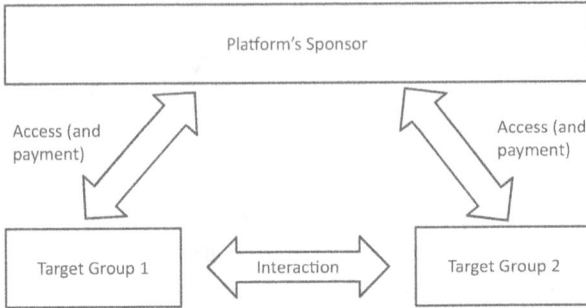

Figure 1.3 Network business model (own illustration)

connect further target groups is referred to as a multisided market or multisided platform. Multisided digital platforms tend to form ecosystems.

The network generates added value by facilitating relationships between the people within the network. The network itself does not necessarily participate in the people's value-creation activity of its users. The network only establishes the connection that creates value for the people. If we take the example of Uber mentioned earlier, the value creation generated by Uber consists of bringing both target groups together. In contrast, the transport service is a value creation that exclusively occurs between people using the Uber network.

The value created by the network, therefore, lies in the interaction. To achieve this, network business models rely on coordination, standardization, conformity, communication, community building, the development of trust and reputation mechanisms, and payment processing. These activities were referred to earlier as governance and summarized in the four C's:

1. Creation: setting up, or programming, an intermediation structure, the software, algorithm, or app. Sometimes, creation is called supply. It is about the main intermediation of the platform or about precisely discerning which target groups interact via the platform.

2. Curation: setting up and enforcing the network's rules. As we will see later, an artificially created network cannot rely on

customs, beliefs, and social institutions. There needs to be a robust design of rules so that people can trust that the intermediation works. Network business models involve strangers. For the intermediation to succeed, the strangers must develop trust in the network. This trust is the result of a set of clear and enforced rules.

3. Customization: engineering the benefits for the users of the network. Each user in each target group uses the network for very personal reasons. The more the user can adapt the network to their specific needs, the higher the likelihood of continuously transacting via the network.

4. Consumption: steering users of the network to interact via the network. In different networks, there is a tendency to use the platform to gain information. Once there is information, the transaction is conducted directly, that is, without the network as an intermediator. I could use a hotel platform to inform myself but then book directly with the hotel for a better price. Consumption means that the network business models engineer the implementation architecture around incentivizing the users to complete the transactions via the platform.

A successful network business model has one apparent attribute: It capitalizes on network effects. A general definition of these effects is:

Network business models are aimed at several target groups that mutually complement each other and create value through the intermediation of the network. In this context, there are two effects:

1. The more people who use the network, the greater the benefits for the individual agents in the network. This constitutes the direct network effect.

2. The larger a target group is, the more benefits the network can generate for the other target groups if successful intermediation

> between the groups is achieved. This constitutes the indirect network effect.

It is helpful to look at some examples of network business models.

- Weekly markets, as a non-digital network business model: The market (place) controls the network. One target group consists of people who want to buy food, and the other consists of people who want to sell food. The network capitalizes on indirect effects; the more different grocers selling the products in the market, the higher the benefits for those buying food. Inversely, the more people come to buy food, the more incentive for grocers to make their produce available in this market.
- Free newspaper, which can be digital or non-digital: The newspaper and its editorial activities sponsor the network. One target group comprises the people who place adverts, and the other comprises those who read the newspaper and, consequently, the adverts. The indirect effect is that the more people read the newspaper, the more interesting it is for people to place ads. However, the more agents place ads, the more the newspaper can do for good editorial staff and stories, increasing the readers' benefits.
- Credit cards are another example of a hybrid network business model: The institution issuing a specific credit card is the platform sponsor, for example, Visa. One target group is those seeking consumer credit. Another target group is made up of people who want to sell goods. There are other target groups, such as financial institutions that grant loans or other sales channels that publicize credit cards. Credit cards are a good example of multisided markets.
- Xbox, a digital platform: Microsoft develops and programs the Xbox game console, assuming the sponsor role. The platform's target groups are people developing games for the Xbox and people playing games. The more game developers and games

there are, the more attractive the platform is for gamers and vice versa.

- Coursera: The digital platform connects people wanting to learn on the one side and people offering courses on the other.

1.7 Types of Network Business Models

The previous section, distinguishing between pipeline and network business models, should not be taken to imply that all network business models are the same. The opposite is true: Every business model is unique. Because of this great diversity, comparing them by grouping them into different types makes sense.

Typification is as tricky as ranking since it is an exercise in discretion. But its purpose is to give an overview. Typification is not about analyzing or understanding individual business models but allows comparisons between them. Since there are several interesting features to compare, typifying platform business models in different, concurrent, or complementary ways helps compare them and understand their common characteristics and differences.

We will go through five typologies, briefly discussing their pros and cons. They are:

1. Channel: Does the network function digitally, non-digitally, or is it a hybrid? The last section used this typification in its example.
2. Purpose: Should the network facilitate individual transactions or comprehensive innovations, if not both?
3. Content: What is the subject of the transactions processed over the network?
4. Interaction: Does the network promote the formation of additional networks and subnetworks?
5. Person: From which perspective is the business model typified, the person using the network or the person controlling the network?

Let us go through the list of typologies starting by the *channel*:

- Offline or non-digital networks aim to engineer the intermediation primarily in direct person-to-person contact without digital tools being constitutive to them. Flea markets and business networks serve as examples here.
- Online or digital networks intermediate constitutively using telecommunications, specifically the internet. Yahoo or eBay are examples of this.
- Hybrid networks combine online and offline possibilities, usually allowing members to choose how to use them. Some service clubs offer these possibilities.

The strength of this typology is the distinction between channels and technologies. The weakness is that this distinction is becoming increasingly blurred. Even traditional offline platforms, such as grocery markets, are including more digital tools in their transactions.

Typification by *purpose*:

- Transaction networks: They aim to facilitate exchange relationships between people using the network to make connections. Examples include Tencent, Tinder, and Airbnb.
- Innovation networks: These networks provide technology and resources so that people using the network can use them to develop new things. Examples of this are Microsoft, Salesforce, and SAP.
- Integrated networks: They facilitate transactions and provide technologies and resources. Examples include Facebook, Xiaomi, and the Apple ecosystem.

This typification provides a substantive indication of how networks function and why people use them. The disadvantage is that the three types are broad, which leads to very large clusters. A finer-grained way of comparing platforms is to typify them according to their content.

Typification by *content*:

- services such as Lyft or Kayak;
- products such as Etsy or Amazon;

- social networking such as LinkedIn or X;
- browser such as Chrome or Firefox;
- development such as Oracle or Google Play;
- payment systems such as PayPal or stripe;
- crowdfunding such as Kickstarter or SeedInvest;
- content providers such as Netflix or Kindle.

This typification focuses on the specific exchange relationships managed through the network. On the one hand, this is informative and demonstrates the variety of network business models. On the other hand, this typification yields very granular distinctions, meaning that the clusters are too small. Platforms want their users to interact. Therefore, a typification by the type of interaction can be helpful.

Typification by *interaction*:

- Network business models are based on interaction and inter-mediation. Digital networks, particularly—but not exclusively—can involve the formation of additional or subnetworks. When parts of a network become autonomous and develop their own dynamics despite being connected to the network, they become an ecosystem.
- A digital ecosystem centers around a digital platform. The platform controls the network to the extent that additional subsystems can establish themselves. These remain connected to the platform, for instance, by using their technology or payment processing while otherwise developing an autonomous dynamic. Operating systems such as iOS, Android, and Microsoft are examples of ecosystems. Ethereum is another example, a network of nodes, smart contracts, decentralized apps, and the cryptocurrency Ether. A person can establish a new platform on these ecosystems, creating their networks and becoming a network provider.

One of the benefits of differentiating between networks as digital platforms and ecosystems lies in the focus on the central attribute of networks, the network effect. The intensity of the interactions that occur through a network depends on how they are described using different network effect models. Digital platforms can be modeled more easily by Metcalfe's law and digital ecosystems by Reed's law. These two laws will be covered later. But this typification also has disadvantages. The reason behind this is that neither Metcalfe nor Reed is empirically applicable. This typification can also have an artificial effect if all digital platforms regard themselves as ecosystems.

Typification by *person*:

- Business model of the person controlling the network, the platform's sponsor: When the network economy is discussed, the focus tends to be on business models from this perspective.
- Business model of the person using the network or user: There is also the perspective of the people using the network to assert their business models. The example of Uber mentioned repeatedly throughout this chapter helps to illustrate this: The sponsor of the digital platform takes on the business model of bringing people together. However, the person offering a journey via Uber wants to drive, that is, to be paid for the journey. People developing apps in digital ecosystems pursue their independent business models. In principle, they have no interest in a particular operating system or app shop but regard participation as a condition for using it to develop their business model, whether it is collecting and selling data, further intermediation, or t-shirts. It is interesting to look at the business models of those using networks, particularly from a business perspective. This aspect, however, is ignored in this textbook.

The benefit of this typification lies in the fact that the respective user intentions come into play. It also points out that not every person in the network has the same intentions and facilitates a combination of network business models (from the perspective of the people controlling the network) and pipeline business models (from the perspective of the people using the platform). The downside of this typification is that it provides limited information on the specific content of the respective business models.

1.8 From the Shift to the Manifesto

Network business models only played a limited role until the break-through of information technology and the internet. Yet, since digital platforms and ecosystems have become widespread, they have triggered economic shifts. Research points to three such shifts:

- Shift in the markets: from the customer's perspective to the target group.
  Network business models shift the focus of a business model to the network's target groups, particularly those using the network to offer their products. There are several reasons for this: These target groups drive the creative interactions on the network, and they usually tend to pay more than others to use the network. The success of the digital platform or ecosystem is frequently closely linked to the number, quality, mutual interdependencies, and so on, of such target groups.
- Shift in competitive benefits: from resources to connections.
  Resources constitute a decisive competitive advantage in pipeline business models. Companies possessing access to good suppliers, employees with above-average qualifications, favorable financing sources, innovative technology, or strategically oriented managers have advantages in their value creation. By contrast, the breadth and diversification of the network give network business models an advantage. The more diversified and complementary the groups that the network connects, the more added value the network as a whole can generate. The breadth and diversification of the network also bring competitive advantages to the people participating in it.
- Shift in value creation: from processes to interactions.
  Value is created in processes in pipeline business models. Each additional process step contributes value to the product or service. A good process organization seeks to organize process steps to lead to optimal value creation. From an economic theoretical point of view, optimum refers to the trade-off between added value and additional costs. Regarding network

business models, value is created through the interactions or transactions performed. The more such transactions there are, the higher the added value. Therefore, the requirement in network economics is to maximize the number of interactions.

Some perceive these changes to be so strong that they assert that the network economy is a new paradigm for how the entire economy will be organized. A paradigm refers to a fundamental way of thinking.

The economist Sangeet Paul Choudary has even published a *Platform Manifesto*. His 16 assertions aim to demonstrate how online platforms and ecosystems are fundamentally transforming the economy as organizational principles. The manifesto is subtitled: "Why Current Business Principles Will Not Function in a Network Economy." He says (Choudary et al. 2015):

1. The ecosystem is the new warehouse.
2. The ecosystem is the new value chain.
3. The network effect is the new economy of scale.
4. Data is the new dollar.
5. Community management is the new human resources management.
6. Liquidity management is the new disposition.
7. Curation and reputation are the new quality management.
8. User journeys are the new sales channels.
9. Distribution is the new location.
10. Behavioral design is the new loyalty program.
11. Data science is the new business model optimization.
12. Social feedback is the new sales commission.
13. Algorithms are the new decision makers.
14. Real-time customization is the new market research.
15. Plug and play is the new business development.
16. The unseen hand is the new iron fist.

Of course, the manifesto needs critical scrutiny. It is written so bombastically that it should be better understood as a provocation. Economic theory, in particular, can reveal some assertions to be simply false (4. Data is the new dollar). Empirical research, on the other hand, reveals that others are very daring (12. Social feedback is the new sales commission).

The manifesto is nevertheless interesting in at least two aspects. First, it reflects the mindset of many people involved in the network economy. Second, it explains broadly which trends are being reinforced by network business models. As food for thought, the manifesto can be taken seriously.

1.9 Controversies

The spread of network business models is causing economic shifts. Provocations like the *Platform Manifesto* highlight how these shifts could continue. Their tone is one of mission consciousness, which has generated controversy. Public discourse and economic research attempt to assess the advantages and opportunities the network economy offers against its disadvantages and risks.

Concerns raised about digital platforms and ecosystems, in particular, include the following:

- Some pipeline business models allege networks of unfair competition. There are even some calls for banning individual networks. Uber, for example, is not allowed to operate in all German cities. The reason behind this is the perceived inequality compared to traditional taxi companies.
- A variety of platforms are banned in California. The justification is that such business models distort the labor market and encourage new dependencies. The chairman of the Federation of German Trade Unions warned of *modern slavery* being created by platforms in 2018.
- In 2021, the European Commission proposed regulating large digital platforms separately. The Commission aims to call these platforms *gatekeepers*. A gatekeeper is a person who can decide on the access of other actors to digital networks.

- Economic theory itself has reservations. It is controversial whether digital platforms and ecosystems are a further development of the network economy. Likewise, there is debate about whether the network economy can fulfill the potential for change, as outlined in the last section.

Conversely, a great deal of potential can also be recognized in the network economy, as the following examples illustrate:

- Digital platforms have demonstrated their ability to contribute to the security of supply during the COVID-19 pandemic. Take, for example, food delivery, contact tracing, working from home, distance learning, and so on. It can also be seen that in many markets into which platforms have penetrated, prices have fallen or been differentiated, and the quality of products and services has increased.
- More than just a few employees use digital platforms to achieve emancipation from gainful employment and increase self-determination. Networks and platforms open up the path to self-employment or facilitate greater freedom in the organization of everyday life.
- The network economy is dynamic. Companies that seem so dominant today that they are labeled as gatekeepers may disappear from the market tomorrow. Myspace seemed dominant only around 15 years ago, and Facebook was the outsider.
- The concerns expressed by economic theory can even be parried. Even though economics has not yet found a generally accepted model for network effects, these effects are real. So, it is the task of economic theory to investigate them in greater depth until they can be modeled. Few fields of research are currently as fruitful as this one.

It would, therefore, be an illusion to expect the discussion about the network economy to subside any time soon. All new things trigger controversy. As things evolve, the discussions tend to increase rather than decrease. Even electrification was controversial at first. It took more than 100 years before people no longer wanted to undo it. Industrialization was controversial, and question marks still surround it today. Ironically, network business models most vociferously criticized the rise of the vertically integrated enterprise with the pipeline business model in the 17th and 18th centuries (Mokyr 2018).

1.10 Critical Assessment

From the perspective of economic theory, whether the network economy is old or new is irrelevant. It is here to stay. It is characterizing reality and changing (part of) the economy. This alone makes it necessary to engage with it.

Speculating about whether the future belongs to it or not is presumptuous. This is because, ultimately, only people acting in an entrepreneurial capacity can answer this question—and in the first instance, only individually and subjectively. This is done by establishing and implementing corresponding business models. Whether and how their calculated bet pans out can only be answered individually and over time.

It is entirely misguided to make the network economy subordinate to the political will. For example, in the European Union and increasingly in the United States, competition authorities increasingly think that digital networks distort competition. In these and other jurisdictions, networks are charged with bending the rules, such as labor markets, and creating social costs. These arguments do not seem to hold. Instead, they have a political target, which is to regulate networks. Regulation of digital and any other platforms, however, is economically harmful.

Economic development, particularly competition, relies on experimentation with new things and questioning the boundaries and rules. Networks are formed to reduce transaction costs. Digital networks cut them even more. They lower transaction costs by laying down different, more straightforward rules. In doing so, rules, especially regulations, often incur transaction costs. This means that when individual business models discover ways of reducing transaction costs through networks, they are acting competitively. The network is specifically a vector for innovation and competition because it questions or overturns existing rules and regulations. Genuine competition involves the ongoing dismantling of organizations and institutions that have been rendered obsolete, especially regulations.

Comparing network business models with the labor market is no less disingenuous. Claiming that network business models make it possible to bypass the labor market is a fallacy. After all, networks and the labor market constitute alternative forms of organization. If you are in one, you are not in the other. Therefore, people using networks to get jobs seek the opposite of employment in the labor market. They want to operate at their own risk and retain their flexibility. It is precisely the intention of these people acting in this manner to turn away from the pipeline business model (with the labor market) and turn their capabilities into added value together with other people in the network business model.

If we look at it from the perspective of economic theory, the enthusiasm surrounding networks is also misguided. There is no disputing that some digital platforms and ecosystems are very successful. Yet this does not mean that all such business models will be successful, nor that only such business models will survive. Keep in mind that most business models that are brokered by networks are pipelines. Consequently, network business models hinge on the success of the pipeline business models they connect. Looking at it less polemically, we could say that pipelines and networks are complementary phenotypes of the division of labor in specialized economies.

Caution is generally advised when it comes to exaggeration. Take, for example, the statement "Data is the new dollar" in the *Platform Manifesto*, where it is an exaggeration. That is why it is also wrong. Data plays a vital role in networks, especially digital platforms and ecosystems. It is necessary on the one hand as it helps or is even essential in controlling the network. It is also important because it can be sold. In other words, it is not a new dollar; it can be turned into dollars.

Well, if neither the political controversies nor the general promises of the network economy are of interest from the perspective of economic theory, what is interesting in their context? What is the economic research program regarding network business models?

The core of network economics is network effects. Researching suitable models for this still needs to be done. More in-depth research into these effects will provide an explanation and understanding of the value creation, pricing, possible business models based on them, and even the potential economic shifts that they bring. While models already exist today, they are constantly undergoing further development.

The governance of networks, particularly digital ecosystems, is of particular interest—and still little researched. It encompasses the game's rules within the ecosystem, technical standardization, intellectual property, and the corresponding opening up of technologies and interfaces to others.

The role played by data management in digital platforms and ecosystems is also not yet well understood. Data are essential for the network economy but not always equally crucial for everyone. In addition, the term *data* remains unclear.

Last but not least, the relationship between the economic and organizational principles of market and network still needs clarification, which can be roughly explained in two ways: One approach states that the market and networks are opposed forms of organization for economic exchange. In other words, to exchange something, you must opt for the market or the network as an exchange vehicle. The second approach is that the market and the network complement each other. Exchange is possible by combining the market principle with the network concept. This approach can be taken further: maybe the market is a network, even a special one. Supply and demand are linked in the market so that they complement each other and find a match for their preferences. The market brings about an exchange relationship. The market, therefore, also makes use of intermediation as a means of transforming opportunities for interaction into concrete transactions.

This textbook sets out this economic research program and the current state of theory in its various chapters. It sidesteps the controversies and political discussions in doing so.

Summary

- A network refers to the reciprocal interaction of different people who are dependent on each other.
- A network economy is a network of interactions used by the people participating to achieve economic goals.
- A platform is a network business model controlled by one person, the sponsor.
- An ecosystem is a controlled link between several interaction structures based on a digital network but promotes additional and subnetworks.
- A network's control function includes managing four central connection types: creation, curation, customization, and consumption.
- The objective is to transform potential connections into specific interactions and exchange relationships.
- Non-digital networks function when high transaction costs can be reduced through networks. The more digital networks reduce transaction costs, the more successful they are.
- Pipeline business models are based on the organization of the entire value chain by a company that first defines processes, allocates resources, and controls results.
- Network business models focus on developing interaction opportunities and transforming this potential into genuine exchange relationships through intermediation. They rely on network effects.
- The more people use the network, the more benefits the person can generate from the network. This is what is known as the direct network effect.
- The more significant the target group of a network is, the more benefits the network can generate for the other target groups, provided intermediation between the groups is successful. This is the indirect network effect.
- Digital networks, in particular, are causing shifts in the economy. These affect markets, competitive advantages, and the organization of value creation.

- These shifts result in controversies relating to the spread of network business models. They are primarily polemics, however.
- Outlook: This textbook's chapters focus on specific aspects of network economics: network effects, which address the network's target groups and value proposition; pricing, which discusses how to generate revenues and create value with the network; and governance, which is about the implementation or intermediation architecture.

Review Questions

First Series: Which Statements Are Correct? Which Are Not?

1. Networks are online business models.
2. People who are independent of each other and complement each other come together in network business models so that everyone benefits individually.
3. Transaction costs refer to the production costs of a commodity or the costs that a person incurs in exchanging the commodity.
4. Transaction costs can be minimized but not eliminated.
5. "The success of a network business model hinges on pipeline business models." Discuss this statement—preferably using an example.
6. "CAPEX Refers to the Cost of Capital Investment, and OPEX Refers to the Operational Cost of Financing Such Investments."
7. "Business Models Have Four Dimensions: Target Group, Value Proposition, Service Architecture, and Revenue Mechanisms."
8. "Business Models Involve Calculated Bets; the Business Person Can Never Know in Advance Whether Such a Bet Will Pay Off."
9. "Costs in Network Business Models Gravitate toward Zero."
10. Ecosystems are purely technical systems.

Second Series: Solve the Following Challenges

1. Name three examples of transaction platforms.
2. Name three examples of innovation platforms.

3. Name three examples of integrated platforms.
4. Which user groups are brought together in the following network business models: flea market, newspaper, BlaBlaCar, Tripadvisor, Android?
5. Explain the network effects and lowering of transaction costs in associations.
6. Explain the network effects and lowering of transaction costs in LinkedIn.
7. Where and how does value creation take place at Nintendo? How is it different from a pipeline type of value creation?
8. Where and how does value creation take place at Uber Eats? How is it different from a pipeline type of value creation?
9. Identify digital platforms that have no ecosystems.
10. Identify dimensions of the following business models and categorize if they are pipelines or networks: hair salon, YouTube, railway, club (disco), grammar school.

Third Series: Respond to the Following Questions and Solve the Mini-Case Studies

1. Analyze the competitive situation in and between the iOS and Microsoft ecosystems. Are they *gatekeepers*?
2. How do you assess the *platform manifesto*? What would change in your evaluation if there was an *and* instead of the phrase *is the new*? For example: *data and dollars*.
3. Identify a new business model based on the network economy. Note: Seek activities with high transaction costs and high potential for network effects.
4. Develop the business model dimensions for the business model identified in 3: target groups, value proposition, service architecture, and revenue mechanisms.
5. How can platforms tap into an additional market opportunity from managing user data?
6. Which connection exists between the *sharing economy* and the network economy?

7. Weigh up the advantages and disadvantages of platform business models in the labor market.

8. "The success of a network business model hinges on pipeline business models." Discuss this statement—preferably using an example.

9. Use an example to explain how a pipeline business model can be transformed into a network business model.

10. What do you understand by the governance of a network? Give examples of non-digital and digital networks.

Commented Bibliography

- Choudary, S.P., G.G. Parker, and M. van Alstyne. *Platform Scale: How an Emerging Business Model Helps Startups Build Large Empires With Minimum Investment*, 2015.
  - It is a classic introductory book that turns insights from economic theory into practical advice. Contains the *Platform Manifesto*.
- Gassmann, O., K. Frankenberger, and M. Choudury. *The Business Model Navigator: 55 Models That Will Revolutionise Your Business*, 2020.
  - The standard textbook on business models. Explains the St. Gallen business model in theory and practice.
- Mokyr, J. "The Past and the Future of Innovation: Some Lessons From Economic History." *Explorations in Economic History* 69 (2018), 13–26.
  - Mokyr asks why innovations trigger controversy. Its main point is that controversies are generally not resolved.
- Munger, M.C. *Tomorrow 3.0: Transaction Costs and the Sharing Economy*. Cambridge University Press, 2018.
  - It is an entertaining but well-founded exploration of transaction costs and their transformation through digitalization.
- Schneider, H. *Creative Destruction and the Sharing Economy: Uber as Disruptive Innovation*. Edward Elgar Publishing, 2017.
  - An analysis of the Uber business model and its regulation.

CHAPTER 2

Network Effects

Learning Agenda

The core of network economics lies in network effects. They can be positive or negative, direct or indirect. Most online platforms and ecosystems set up a governance system to ensure positive network effects. Since these effects are dynamic, platform sponsors continuously adapt their governance. This chapter explains network effects. Here, we will use economic theory to model these effects by assessing how they benefit platform sponsors and users. We will also look at specific challenges regarding network effects, the chicken or egg problem, and market polarization. After reading this chapter, you will be able to:

- Section 2.1: describe the economic concept of benefit or utility.
- Section 2.2: model the benefits or utility of connections in networks.
- Section 2.3: differentiate between direct and indirect network effects.
- Section 2.4: operationalize the benefits or utility from networks as functions.
- Section 2.5: apply a realistic model for the benefits of networks.
- Section 2.6: familiarize yourself with network governance.
- Section 2.7: explain the chicken and egg problem in the context of networks.
- Section 2.8: elucidate the idea of economic equilibrium in a network model.

- Section 2.9: discuss market polarization as a possible effect of networks.
- Section 2.10: critically reflect the contents of this chapter.

2.1 Benefit or Utility

The 1908 annual report of AT&T—American Telephone and Telegraph Company—states on page 21:

> A telephone—without a connection at the other end of the line —is neither a toy nor a scientific instrument. It is one of the least useful things in the world. The value of a telephone depends on its connection to other telephones—increasing with the number of connections.

This gets to the heart of the network effect, which occurs when something becomes more helpful to people as the number of people in the same network increases. The last chapter defined the network as several different people who transact using a common infrastructure or interaction structure. It has also been argued that network business models rely on network effects to transform potential relationships into interactions. For this to occur, however, the network's sponsor must intermediate. While the last chapter took a business-centered view of establishing a business model based on networks, this chapter looks at the nuts and bolts of networks, explaining how they work and their inner mechanisms. To accomplish this, this chapter uses economic theory.

Many people—remember: This term includes individuals and companies—use networks to achieve their goals. Knowing these goals in detail is neither valuable nor feasible when explaining networks. What people want is their business. In economics, we need an abstract term that allows us to refer to all personal goals without needing to detail these goals.

Why do people search via DuckDuckGo? Why do they listen to music on Spotify? Why do they post on Reddit? What is people's motivation to rideshare on Juno? Why can we find Pete Seeger's songs on Apple Music? Being active on these platforms, either as a consumer, supplier, or sponsor, benefits them. The benefit can be material, or it can be immaterial, or it can even be a mix.

Economists suppose that people want to increase their benefits by pursuing goals that are beneficial to themselves. This does not say anything about the specific content of the benefit. The claim is comprehensive: People do things they consider beneficial—according to their individual and subjective ideas and standards. Benefit, as a term, fulfills both ends: On the one hand, it allows us to speak about something people want or pursue; on the other, it is sufficiently abstract for us not to discuss its specific content. In economics, instead of benefit, the term *utility* is often used. But, for simplicity, we use the term *benefit* in this book.

Knowing these terms allows us to answer critical questions: Why do people join a network? Why does an entrepreneur sponsor a platform? It is because they consider it beneficial for themselves. While it is up to the individual agent to determine their specific benefit or utility, the benefit is usually influenced by a series of exogenous factors. These are factors outside the control of the person. One of the most important factors is how many other agents compete to use the same resources. Here is a categorization:

- *Excludable benefit:* When someone eats an apple, the benefit is generally accrued individually and only individually, that is, a second person taking a bite off the same apple reduces the first person's benefit. Each additional person who bites into the apple reduces the benefit of that first person. Any additional person biting into the apple negatively benefits the others. An early negative benefit arising from a second user indicates the exclusivity of a good or service. It benefits only one user. The apple provides benefits exclusively to the person eating the apple alone.

- *Indifferent benefit*: Driving a car is another case of individual benefit. Usually, it is not a problem for one driver if another person gets into the same car. A second person getting into the car does not generally lead to any significant change in benefit for the driver. Up to maximum capacity, the driver can drive indifferently of how many others are sitting in the car. The same applies to the number of vehicles. Drivers are usually indifferent to other vehicles if they can drive without hindrance.

- *Decreasing benefit*: However, when there are too many people in a car, that is, more than five, or too many people driving on the roads, causing traffic jams, the benefit of the driver decreases with each additional person who wants to get in or each additional person who wants to drive on the road.

- *Increasing benefit*: In the case of some specific goods and services, the benefit to one person increases when other people use the same commodity. The AT&T example mentioned above made precisely this point about the telephone. More than one user is needed to experience the benefits of the telephone. The more people have a telephone connection, the greater the benefit for those connected via the telephone network.

The idea behind network effects is that they increase the benefit of the people in the network with increasing agents joining the network. However, platform sponsors need to engineer these increasing benefits by setting up a system of governance. Without governance, platforms can crowd out and decrease the benefits to the users, which prompts them to leave. Even indifferent users are not advantageous to the platform. To work, networks need to benefit their users by connecting them.

2.2 Connections Are Benefits

The benefit of a network lies in the number of connections it can generate between people. The generation of connection is called intermediation. An effective network sponsor enables connections leading to exchanges or transactions between the people in the network. Let us think about this using the phone:

- As we have read directly from AT&T, the benefit of a telephone network with one person using the phone is zero. That is because there is no connection with just one person. Zero connections mean zero benefits.

- A connection is possible if a second person uses the phone in the same network. Since there is precisely one connection possible, the benefit of this network is one—we will come back to this metric shortly. It is up to the platform's sponsor, the phone company, to effectively steer these two people to use the connection to exchange information.

- If five people are in the same phone network, the number of possible connections increases to 10. This also means that the benefit of this network is 10.

- Note how the benefit here has increased overproportionately regarding the number of people. Two people have become five. With two people, the benefit, that is, the number of connections, amounted to one. With five people, it is 10. The number of people has increased by a factor of 2.5. The benefit has increased by a factor of 10. This overproportionate rise in benefit lies at the heart of the network effect.

What is with the metric of 1 and 10? Was not the benefit individual and subjective? How can it be measured? And if we are measuring it, what is the unit? This is economics at work. We must choose the best approximations for their inner logic to make relationships explainable. Naturally, benefits cannot be measured because they are individual, subjective, context-sensitive, and unstable. However, to talk about them and show how networks work, we need to use an explanatory device that, at the same time, is simple to understand and captures the essence of the economic phenomenon. This is what we just did in the example.

We took the number of connections as a proxy for the benefit. Economists would say we made the term benefit operational by assigning them a unit of measure. With that unit, we can better compare the benefits of a network with two and one with five people. The metric chosen here, as an explanatory device, is to equal the number of connections to the benefit of the network. With that, we can show how a network's benefit increases with the number of connections made possible. We can also show the core of the network effect, the overproportionate increase in the network's overall benefits with increased users and connections. But we should not fool ourselves into believing that the metric is accurate, objective, or absolute: It is an explanatory device and a proxy.

Back to network effects. What explains the overproportionate increase in benefits? Frequently, economic theory relates network effects to externalities. An *externality* is the consequence of an economic action whose value is not included in the price of the action. There is a distinction between positive and negative externalities:

- *Positive externalities* are generated in networks because the networks create more significant benefits through the linking of their elements, that is, the people who use them. A new person who joins the network increases the benefits for those already connected and makes the network more attractive to others. The theory of externalities tells us that this increase in the overall benefit is not fully compensated. In other words, the person joining is not compensated by the others for the additional benefits they generate.

- *Negative externalities* emerge when the network is saturated or overloaded by an additional person joining. This reduces the benefits for people already participating in the network. The network itself becomes less attractive. The theory of externalities states that this loss of benefit by the additional person joining the network is not fully compensated. The person joining the network does not compensate the others for the loss of benefit caused by their joining.

There are several issues with explaining network effects with externalities. First, the externality theory adds another concept to the already abstract concepts of network benefits and connections. It is better to keep things simple and to operate only with one set of abstractions instead of two, so we will continue to count connections instead of thinking about foregone compensations. Second, the theory of externalities establishes a logical link between benefits and compensation, that is, it assumes that the individual action leads to a specific compensation. This link does not exist; even if it did, it does not apply to networks because compensation in networks follows a different logic. Most of the time, compensation does not go hand in hand with the benefits individual people get or create in the network.

However, there is an insight coming from the theory of externalities. This insight will be significant for our further discussion of networks. It is about benefits and for whom they occur. Benefits occur at two levels. First, it occurs at the level of the individual people in a network or joining it. But they also occur at the level of the whole network. These benefits differ in each case. A functioning network business model can simultaneously increase the benefit for the network and the benefit for the people participating in it. Effective networks create benefits at both levels simultaneously. This is seen as a proxy in the adoption rates of networks. To illustrate this: How long did it take for the following applications to achieve 50 million users?

- Cars   62 years
- Telephones   50 years
- Electricity   46 years
- Credit cards   28 years
- TVs   22 years
- Debit cards   12 years
- Internet   7 years
- PayPal   5 years
- YouTube   4 years
- Facebook   3 years
- Twitter   2 years
- Pokémon Go   19 days

2.3 Direct and Indirect Network Effects

The term *network effects* warrants more explanation. Most networks are multisided, connecting one group of people with another or many others. In this case, we distinguish between direct and indirect and positive and negative effects.

Direct network effects, also known as horizontal network effects or same side effects, occur when a network's benefit increases as more people use it. For example, the more people connected to a phone network, the more benefits the network has; the more people use a document exchange standard, for example, PDF, the higher the benefit.

Indirect network effects, also known as vertical network effects or cross-side effects, arise when at least two different customer groups are intermediated. The benefit of at least one group grows as the other group(s) grow. The groups are complementary. For example, hardware may become more valuable to consumers with the growth of compatible software, or studios make more movies the more people watch them.

Complementary goods are two or more goods typically consumed or used together. In network effects, the term complementary refers to two groups of people using a network complementing each other, for example, the driver and the person who wants to be driven.

Positive network effects: The benefits of the network and the benefits for the person using the network increase when others or other groups join the network.

Negative network effects: The benefits of the network or the benefits for the person using the network diminish when others or other groups join the network.

Some examples were already given when introducing these effects in the box. Let us review some more to better grasp the different effects depending on the platform and its business model:

- The *game console* connects game developers and gamers. Developers' benefits increase as the number of gamers grows, and vice versa. This generates positive indirect network effects for both sides. However, more developers can lead to too much competition within the group of developers, creating a negative direct network effect. Note how the competition between developers is another positive cross-side effect since it benefits gamers, leading to more, newer, and different games. Suppose the platform sponsor increases the gamers' side benefits to a maximum. In that case, they might scare off the developers, prompting them to leave the network and decreasing the gamers' benefits. On the other hand, if the sponsor focuses on increasing the developers' benefits, for example, by allowing exclusivity to some types of games, the gamers might grow frustrated by the lack of diversity of games and leave the platform, which, in turn, decreases the benefits on all sides. The sponsor, therefore, must maintain a balance between the positive indirect effects and the negative direct effects on the developers' side. This balance is the outcome of the governance of the network, a topic further explored in Chapter 4.

- A *newspaper* connects readership and advertisers. Advertisers benefit from a larger readership, which is a positive indirect effect. For readers, the effect of more adverts can be positive, neutral, or negative, depending on individual preferences and how the sponsor uses the revenues from ads. The cross-side effect is positive if the revenue makes the paper cheaper or features better news stories. If it leads to the newspaper being full of ads, making the reading more complicated, it is negative. The direct network effect is neutral for readers since how many others read the newspaper is immaterial to its content. The direct effect can be negative for advertisers, as more advertisers mean higher costs to place an advert and less attention to the individual ad. Again, establishing a balance of all these effects is the aim of the governance instituted by the sponsor.

- A *dating platform* connecting men and women (to reduce the
  scope of the example), with positive indirect effects on both sides
  as the number of participants in the other group grows. As long
  as there is no crowding out, the number of people on the same
  side is irrelevant (in this binary case); therefore, the direct effect
  is neutral. However, there are preoccupations with the quality
  of people in each group. Low quality decreases the indirect
  effect since people from other groups might exit the network.
  It is for the sponsor to maintain the quality level. The story
  changes when there is overcrowding. If too many people are in
  one group, people of that group might exit the network because
  their chances to meet people in the other group are diminished.
  However, people from the other group might also drop out if
  the overcrowding of one group leads to incessant messaging and
  attempts at establishing contact. In both cases, the effects are
  negative. Again, the sponsor's function is to set up a governance
  system safeguarding quality and preventing overcrowding.

These examples assume networks are already big enough (have
attained critical mass) but not too large (have no crowding-out effects).
These are important points which will be discussed later. If networks are
too small, they cannot generate enough connections to create benefits.
Conversely, the overall and individual benefits decrease if they are too
large.

Let us review a three-sided platform like *Facebook* as a final example
of network effects. It connects *three sides*: content users, developers, and
advertising companies.

- Content users create, acknowledge, and comment on content.
  A more extensive user base increases the benefits for other
  content users, which is a direct positive network effect. This
  more extensive base also increases the benefits for the other user
  groups, which are indirect effects.
- Developers receive tools from Facebook to create applications.
  These tools are the application programming interfaces, software

development kits, and integrated development environments. Facebook engineers a specific quality control and standardization level with them while organizing access to its platform. More content users increase the benefits for developers, creating a potential use base for their apps, which is a positive cross-side effect. The effect also holds the other way around: More developers increase the benefits for content users by enabling them to use the platform in more diverse and personalized ways.

• Advertising companies pay Facebook to advertise on the platform and within the ecosystem. Advertising companies want to address as many (personalized) content users and developers as possible. This means that an increase in the size of the other two market sides means an increase in benefits for this market side. Yet the other market sides also benefit from the growth of advertising companies on Facebook. These generate revenue for the platform and ensure its free use for the other sides. These are also indirect, positive network effects. However, advertising companies can also lead to negative direct network effects on Facebook. If more advertising companies use Facebook, their competition becomes more intense. There is also a risk of experiencing the effects of crowding out from advertising companies if advertising becomes so rampant that content users and developers abandon the platform. Additionally, content users and developers might leave the platform if advertising companies flood Facebook with ads or the users flood Facebook with the wrong ads. These would be negative indirect effects.

2.4 Benefit Functions

So far, we have introduced the number of potential connections in a network as a proxy for benefit. We have also reviewed how these connections benefit the people in a network and the different types of network effects. In the next step, we will formalize the notion of benefit and see how the network effect can be operationalized. For this step, we need to understand models and functions.

Economic theory aims to describe network effects and model them. Modeling is, in many ways, the core of economics as a science. A model is a simplified cause-effect mechanism seeking to explain the inner logic of an economic phenomenon. Again, here, we need to be careful. The economic model is not a claim to reality. It is a logical claim, a tool to make sense of something that occurs repeatedly. It is an explanatory device intended to make a relationship understandable.

Economic models are usually written as analytical relationships between variables, that is, functions. A function starts with the variable that needs to be explained, the so-called dependent variable. This variable is explained using other variables, which are called independent variables. Let us use some of the terms introduced in this book to see how they relate to variables:

- Benefit: The benefit is what people want when using platforms. The benefit is, therefore, the outcome of the network and, consequently, the dependent variable—the one to be explained. The benefit can take two forms: It is, on the one hand, the overall benefit of the network. As such, it is labeled here as U (upper case). On the other hand, there is the benefit of the person participating in the network. For this purpose, it is labeled as u (lowercase).

- People: People look for connections in networks. In this context, the number of people in the network facilitates the creation of these connections, leading to benefits. The number of participants explains the number of connections and, therefore, the benefit created by a network. The number of people in the network constitutes the explanatory or independent variable. The number of people using the network is labeled n (lowercase).

- Effectiveness: Connections are established in networks, and the network controls them through intermediation. How effective this intermediation is can also explain how the benefit is realized. Therefore, this effectiveness of intermediation can also act as an explanatory or independent variable. In the following, it is only used as an example and is labeled with e (lowercase). Effectiveness is the variable associated with how well the platform's governance works. The value for *e* is between 0 and 1. One signifies a maximally effective governance, converting all possible connections into exchange transactions. Zero stands for maximally ineffective intermediation, impeding any possible connection from materializing in a transaction.

The model of the benefit of a network is expressed analytically in a benefit function. This function is generic, that is, it establishes a relationship between the variables just explained. This relationship is easy to understand. The overall benefit of the network is a function of the number of people using this network and the effectiveness of intermediation in this network:

$$U = f\ (n, e)$$

Written as this, we still cannot say anything precise about the function. We only know that benefit is a function of the number of people and the effectiveness of the intermediation. But how does the number of people influence the benefit exactly? For this, we need to operationalize the function. The abstract function gives us the elements; the operationalization tells us how these elements are linked.

One way of operationalizing is to go back to computer science. There are already several ideas of how networks operate in computer science. We can borrow these ideas and interpret them with economic theory. The best-known ideas of operationalizing networks in computer science are the *laws* of Sarnoff, Metcalfe, and Reed. We can transform them into economic benefit functions. In addition to those three, another way to model the network effect is to consider the deceleration of the network effect. Let us review these four options.

Sarnoff's law states that the overall benefit of a network is proportional to the number of people using the network. The benefit per person corresponds to their relationship to the network. Now, we need to transform this *law* of computer science into a formal economic model by developing a benefit function, such as:

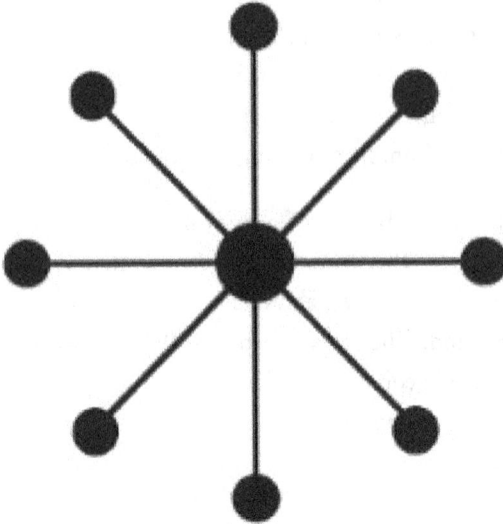

Figure 2.1 Network according to Metcalfe's law (own illustration)

$$U = n$$

$$u = 1$$

Figure 2.1 illustrates the principle behind Sarnoff's law. A network provider is at the center of the network. The people using the network are connected to that center. They are not connected to each other. The more people joining the network, the greater the overall benefit of the network in proportion to the number of people joining. Yet the benefit for the person stays the same. It arises from their connection with the network provider. Examples include TV channels and radio stations, which only broadcast or rebroadcast programs, that is, they have no advertising or interaction with the people in the network.

Metcalfe's law states that the benefit of a network increases approximately by the square of the number of additional people who participate in the network. The benefit per person is the first derivative of the overall benefit. Again, we transform this general *law* into a formal economic model:

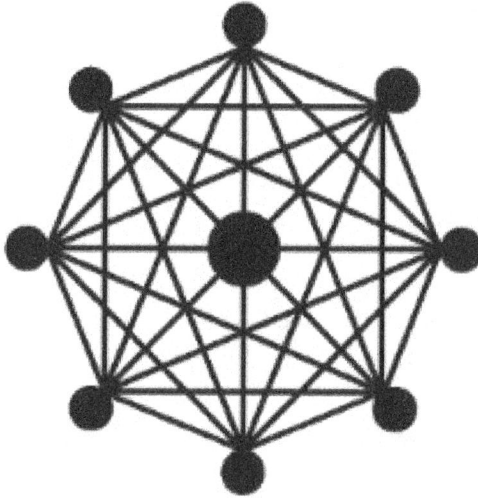

Figure 2.2 Network according to Metcalfe's law (own illustration)

$$U = n^2 - n$$

$$u = 2n - 1$$

Figure 2.2 illustrates the principle behind Metcalfe's law. Individual people can connect via the network and, therefore, get in touch with each other. An additional person joining the network increases the number of possible connections. This increases benefits for the entire network by the square of the number of new members. The benefit for the person in the network increases by the number of additional connections that can be created by joining. Telephone networks and email are good examples of this.

For large networks, Metcalfe's law can be simplified:

$$U = n^2$$

$$u = 2n$$

Metcalfe's law can also accommodate the effectiveness of the intermediation by adding variable e to the function:

$$U = (n^2 - n)\, e$$

In this case, the benefit function is modified so that a network's overall benefit is the product of its size, factoring in the effectiveness of the intermediation. You can see that the overall benefit is zero if e is 0, no matter how many potential connections. If e is 1, all the potential connections will yield a transaction.

Reed's law states that the benefit of a network grows overproportionate to the number of subnetworks that can form within the network. In other words, this involves the formation of groups and the possibility of group connections within a network. Again, it can be expressed as a formal economic model:

$$U = 2^n - n - 1$$

$$u = 2n - 1$$

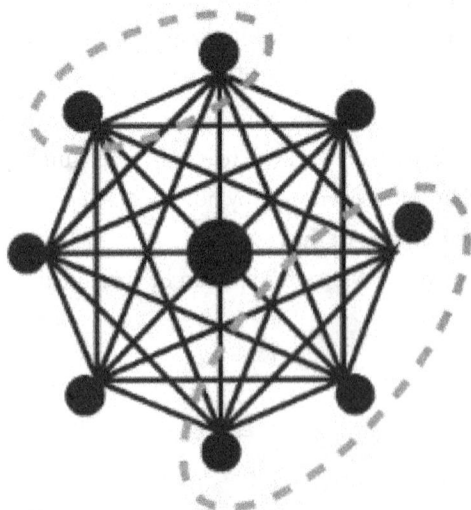

Figure 2.3 Network according to Reed's law (own illustration)

Figure 2.3 illustrates the principle behind Reed's law. Individual users use the network to exchange information, establish groups, and exchange information within these groups. The overall benefit of the network is overproportionate to new members since each new member increases both the possibilities for connections and the formation of groups. The benefits also increase for the individuals who participate in the network. Examples of this include social networks and chat forums.

This model, too, can incorporate the effectiveness of intermediation:

$$u = (2^n - n - 1)\, e$$

Slowing down or deceleration of the network effect: There is also the possibility that the network effects will slow down after a certain amount of people join the network. This is reflected in a logarithmic benefit function of the form:

$$U = n * \log(n)$$

The network's benefits might be slowed down due to unequal benefits for the individual participants. Another reason for this could be limited group formation and, consequently, limited opportunities for connection. Friction in the network may also result in a decrease in dynamics. In such a case, the benefit continues to increase overproportionately, but not at the rate (better: exponents) that Metcalfe and Reed envisage.

2.5 A Nuanced Model

Transforming ideas stemming from computer science into economic models gives us a first notion of how platforms generate benefits depending on the number of users and the effectiveness of the intermediation. However, Sarnoff's, Metcalfe's, and Reed's laws and the functions based on them that we developed apply to individual, specific networks. We need a more nuanced model to describe and understand networks in general. As hinted several times before, the network's development over time, or better, with the increase in its reach, is

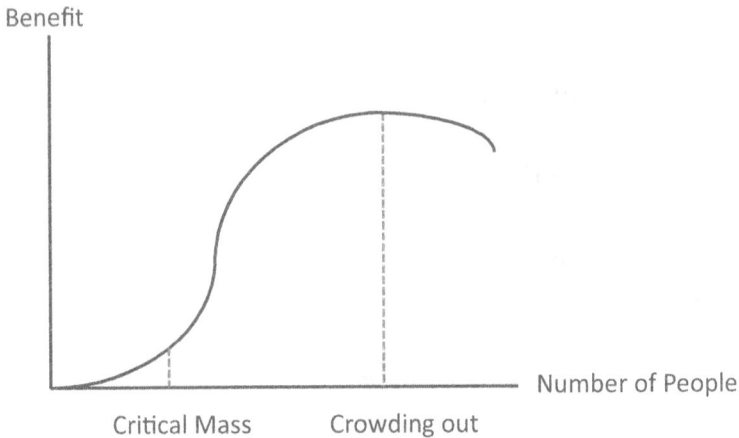

Benefit

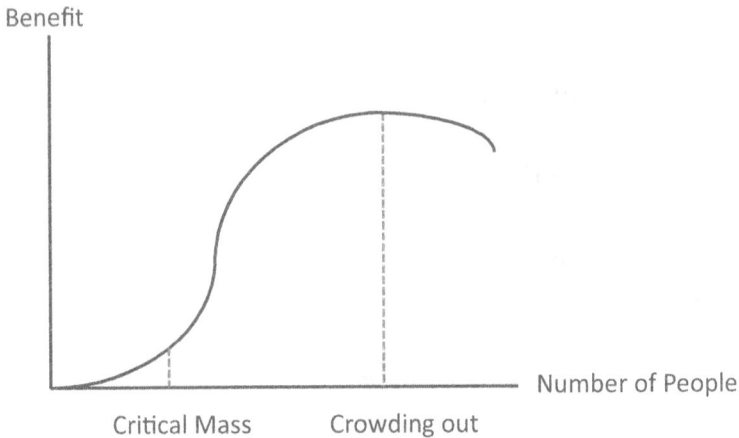

Number of People

Critical Mass   Crowding out

Figure 2.4 Benefit function of a network with four phases (own illustration)

essential for nuance. They, too, go through phases, each with a different function. We will now introduce a model with four phases.

Figure 2.4 illustrates this four-phase process, which will be explained in more detail below. It shows the network's benefit as the dependent variable, explained by the number of people using it as the independent variable. The figure's function is simplified to only one variable to explain the benefit function. But of course, a third axis for *e*, the other independent variable, can be added to the graph.

The curve is the graphical rendering of the function. The first phase shows it close to the origin until it reaches the critical mass. Its course concave up is already apparent. This concavity up becomes more pronounced in the second phase until the inflection point. After that, the curve becomes concave down, indicating a new phase of diminishing marginal network effects. The fourth and last phase is reached when the curve starts to slope downwards, indicating a crowding out or saturation of the network and, therefore, a loss of benefits.

Let us review the phases in more detail with their distinct markers:

1. From zero users to critical mass: The first people using the
    network only generate minor network effects. They are too few,
    connected in a small club and interacting among themselves.

The network effects and benefits are low until the critical mass threshold is passed. However, the growth rate of the network is high since each new person joining the network considerably increases the benefits of the incumbents by expanding their possibilities of interacting. In this phase, the function is concave up, that is, the benefit grows overproportionate to the number of new users.

2. From the critical mass to the inflection point: When crossing the critical mass threshold, the function follows metcalfe's or reed's laws. The function becomes more concave up, meaning that the growth of the network benefit is most substantial in this phase. Because of the existing number of people using the network, each new user exponentially increases connecting possibilities.

3. From the inflection point to the crowding out: After the inflection point, the function's course becomes concave down, pointing to the decreasing marginal benefit of another person joining the network. Each additional person joining the network leads to an increasingly underproportionate (but still positive) increase in benefits. Maybe these new entrants are not as interesting to the network as those before them were. Maybe they make the network too complicated to navigate. The function becomes logarithmic in this phase because the network effect is decelerating.

4. After the crowding out: If the network grows so large that the people crowd each other out, that is, If the network reaches saturation, the benefit decreases due to negative network effects.

Naturally, the function in Figure 2.4 can be expressed analytically. However, consistent with the idea of that ioffering an introductory textbook, the explanation of the graphic suffices to understand the nuance added by a four-phased model. More important than the mathematical—or algebraic—formula of the function are the main takeaways of this more advanced model.

Takeaways: How Do Network Effects Work?

- A network produces benefits at two levels: at the level of the person using the network and at the aggregated network level. The benefit of a network is primarily contingent on the number of people using the network.
- The benefit of a network is also influenced by the effectiveness of its sponsor in intermediating.
- Functioning networks operate between the critical mass and the saturation point when crowding out occurs.
- The benefit function of a network can be modeled in different ways, some operationalizing *laws* of computer science, like Sarnoff's, Metcalfe's, or Reed's, and some more nuanced.
- A nuanced model allows the function to change according to the network's phase. In its inception and especially after achieving critical mass, the benefit function is concave up, increasing overproportionately to new people entering the network. After the inflection point, the function becomes concave down, showing the deceleration of network effects. With saturation, the benefits decrease because of negative network effects.
- In practice, each network has its own critical mass and saturation point (if any).
- Finally, with the development of a network, its configuration of phases can change.

2.6 Network Governance

This book mentioned already that the platform's sponsor job is to intermediate. As a business model, this entails setting up the platform and leading the network members to interact via the platform. The sponsor cannot trust economic theory, thinking that the mere number of people automatically entails transactions. For those network effects to kick in and unfold, the sponsor must effectively intermediate

—remember variable *e*. Effective intermediation is the result of an appropriate system of network governance. The sponsor must set this up and continually adapt it to the network dynamics.

As mentioned above, governance can be thought of along the four C's:

1. Creation: setting up, or programming, an intermediation structure, the software, algorithm, or app. Sometimes, creation is called supply. It is about the main intermediation of the platform or about precisely discerning which target groups interact via the platform.

2. Curation: setting up and enforcing the network's rules. As we will see later, an artificially created network cannot rely on customs, beliefs, and social institutions. There needs to be a robust design of rules so that people can trust that the intermediation works. Network business models involve strangers. For the intermediation to succeed, the strangers must develop trust in the network. This trust is the result of a set of clear and enforced rules.

3. Customization: engineering the benefits for the users of the network. Each user in each target group uses the network for very personal reasons. The more the user can adapt the network to their specific needs, the higher the likelihood of continuously transacting via the network.

4. Consumption: steering users of the network to interact via the network. In different networks, there is a tendency to use the platform to gain information. Once there is information, the transaction is conducted directly, that is, without the network as an intermediator. I could use a hotel platform to inform myself but then book directly with the hotel for a better price. Consumption means that the network business models engineer the implementation architecture around incentivizing the users to complete the transactions via the platform.

The four C's suffice as an explanation for governance in terms of the business model. Assessing governance from the perspective of economic theory goes a step further. Based on the logic of the four C's, economic theory develops, again, a model with a function. If the network's benefit function represents the demand side, the governance function is the supply side.

U (and u) are the benefits the demand side expects from the network. The supply side's benefit is mainly the payoff that the supplier or sponsor of the network expects. This payoff is a function of how many people join and use the network. Let us call the supply side function S for supply or sponsor, and since it is dependent on the number of users, let us call this number here: q. In this case, the function of the sponsor's benefit is:

$$S = f(q)$$

This is a barebones representation of a logical and intuitive relationship. The more users in a network, the higher the benefits and payoffs for its sponsor. As before, the function needs operationalization. The specific platform's business model does this and leads to a curve with a changing slope, as shown in Figure 2.5.

This graph, too, explains the benefit as a function of the number of people. In this case, though, the benefit of the network's sponsor is

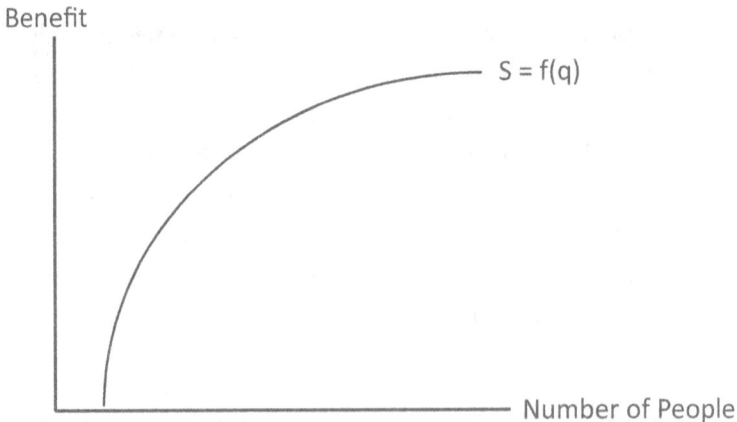

Figure 2.5 *Supply curve of a network business model (own illustration)*

plotted. Its slope is steep in the beginning and becomes increasingly flat. Let us review the—in this case, three—phases of supply:

1. From zero to the steepest slope: The network sponsor implements a business model that attracts people to transact via the platform, reaching the critical mass as quickly as possible. The steepness of the slope will depend on how quickly people join the network, which again depends on the uniqueness of the value proposition, the efficiency of the implementation, and, most probably, the platform's marketing.

2. Flattening of the curve. In functioning networks, demand leads to more demand because of the network effects: If a network functions, it is sufficiently attractive to draw in additional people to join it. As the network grows, more and more governance is needed, which trades off against the sponsor's benefit, leading to a less steep curve. In this phase, governance needs to be continuously adjusted to keep up with the dynamics of those people using the network.

3. Flat curve. When the network becomes too complicated to control or when crowding out happens, the sponsor only has legacy benefits and cannot incur new benefits for themselves.

Again, this is a stereotypical rendering of the supply curve. It nonetheless explains how benefits change for the platform's sponsor depending on the network's dynamic, which goes hand in hand with the number of persons in a network. Governance deals with these dynamics, establishing a trade-off between the different aspects of the network.

According to economic theory, the next step is to put supply and demand in the same graph, equaling both functions and looking for an equilibrium. However, before completing that step, let's review the *chicken and egg problem*: How a network reaches the critical mass.

2.7 Chicken and Egg Problem

How can a platform offer a value proposition without people using the network? At the beginning of any network, no people use them because they are new. But how can the network bring people in?

For multisided business models in which one side is buyers and the other sellers, the chicken and egg problem refers to attracting sides to the platform. The problem arises because buyers will not use the platform if there are not enough products or services, and sellers will not join if there are not enough buyers.

The best economic theory can do is point out the problem. Only business practice can solve it. And indeed, some solutions require a portion of shrewdness:

- *Take over one side of the market yourself.* The network's sponsor assumes the function of a market side until there are enough people on the other side to make the network attractive. Amazon initially adopted the seller side until it had enough buyers. In other words, by assuming one side of the market, Amazon became a retailer, a pipeline business model. Only when the buyers' group became large enough did Amazon become attractive to sellers. And only then could it specialize in intermediating transactions, becoming a full network business model.

- *Fake it until you make it.* Some platforms pretend—at least initially—to have enough users on both sides. These networks also pretend to intermediate while, in reality, just matching their own supply to whichever demand they find. The freelancing platform Upwork, for example, allows companies to book self-employed workers for specific jobs. It started by manually recruiting workers to get as many participants as possible onto the marketplace. This is also a pipeline model. When user numbers increased later, they could automate the intermediation processes and stop recruiting, allowing people to join the network and seek its intermediation.

- *Push or subsidize a side with extras*: This tactic aims to generate additional benefits for the seller. This is a usual approach for business-to-consumer platforms. The Californian catering platform OpenTable, for example, which offers online reservations for tables in restaurants, was able to increase its coverage with this strategy. OpenTable initially struggled to find a critical mass of participating restaurants. The platform operators quickly recognized that they had to offer restaurants an additional benefit to attract more business. This is why they introduced a digital restaurant reservation book, allowing restaurant operators to build a digital guest database. They also automated invoicing. Later, they added a web-based version to their app, which helped them win over more restaurants. The first Uber rides were subsidized. The side that wanted a ride received vouchers at hotels and restaurants. They used these vouchers to pay for the ride.

- *Gain aggregators*: Aggregators refer to physical locations such as large companies with a high concentration of potential platform participants and where information spreads quickly by word of mouth. Platform sponsors can identify such locations to attract many participants to a platform. Such a strategy is particularly suitable for peer-to-peer platforms. The U.S. ride-sharing company Zimride—the equivalent of the European BlaBlaCar—initially struggled to establish trust between drivers and those searching for a ride. This is why Zimride targeted universities. This allowed the platform to reach many users at once and build trust between drivers and those searching for a lift, as students trust their fellow students more than strangers. This strategy, coupled with a rating system, helped Zimride to grow rapidly.

- *Linking up or free riding*: This tactic relies on *platform layering*. A platform deliberately links content from other platforms to reach more people. Emphasizing user-friendliness may even succeed in creating added value compared to these platforms. The accommodation provider Airbnb relied heavily on this strategy at the beginning and, for example, featured listings from Craigslist, a well-known American ad website, on its website with a significantly more pleasant user experience and a better search filter.

- *Sharpen the focus*: Many digital platforms focus on certain areas, social niches, or specific industries to achieve a critical mass. It is possible with this strategy to reach a critical mass quickly, even in competitive markets, as supply and demand in the target group can be better regulated. For example, Uber's ride-hailing started focusing on San Francisco and gradually expanded to other cities. Since network effects occur locally at Uber, it was decisive for the platform to grow the number of drivers and those searching for a ride simultaneously. For example, it would be of little use to a passenger in San Francisco if a driver was available in New York. Many start-ups specialize in a particular industry niche. Whether tradespeople, babysitters, or gardeners—every industry now has a specific platform.

Economic equilibrium is a state in which economic forces are balanced. When equilibrium is reached, economic variables remain unchanged without external influences. Economic equilibrium is also called market equilibrium, in which the demand function equals the supply function. Equilibrium is important in most economic models because it enables an analysis of the state and outcomes of markets.

2.8 Equilibrium in Networks

Do equilibria exist in networks? This question is at the heart of a controversial debate. Some economists say that the network economy is so dynamic that there can be no equilibrium. Variables change too often too quickly. On the other hand, what would a network in equilibrium

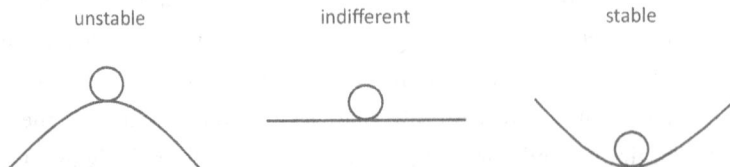

Figure 2.6 Types of equilibrium (own illustration)

look like, and is there anything to learn from it? This compound question merits being addressed.

Let us start by differentiating types of equilibria. In equilibrium, variables do not change because they are stable. But how stable is this state? There are three types of equilibria, as Figure 2.6 points out.

While all three pictures represent equilibria, each is different and has a different reaction to exogenous factors, influences from outside the model's function:

1. Even the most minor changes can upset an *unstable equilibrium*, making the ensuing unbalanced change disproportionate to the effect.
2. An *indifferent equilibrium* can be brought out of balance, but the resulting unbalanced change is proportional to the acting effect.
3. A *stable equilibrium* can be brought out of balance but tends to return to equilibrium following the change.

Now, we need to apply the idea of equilibrium to networks. We need the benefit and supply functions discussed in the prior subsections. They are the demand and supply functions in network models. Having them in the same graph means we can look for the intersection points of the U and S functions. We would expect these to be equilibria. Figure 2.7 plots U and S along the same axis: benefits of the network and the number of people using the network.

As in Figures 2.4 and 2.5, the benefit of the network is explained by the number of people in that network. The dashed line denotes the benefit function U. The four-phase model in Figure 2.4 has been simplified to a straight line for simplicity's sake. This benefit function reflects the demand for the network, that is, the benefit that the network users on all sides of the intermediation derive from the network. The network supply function S is the continuous curve. It shows the benefits for the network's sponsor, which arise from the number of people in the network and their willingness to continue sponsoring it. In this version, both are functions of people using the network. In the figure, there are three points marked with a circle:

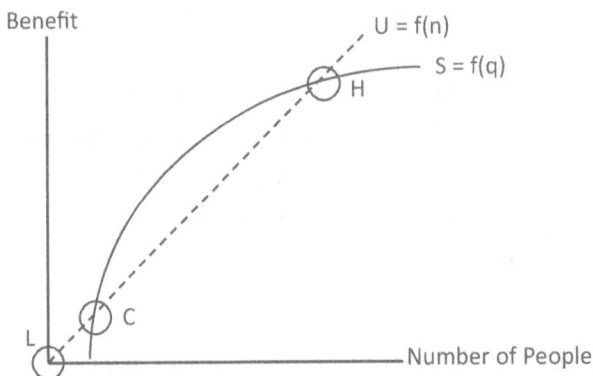

Figure 2.7 Equilibria in networks (own illustration)

1. Point L is the origin. No people are using the network there, and there are no benefits. L is a stable equilibrium.

2. Point C is an equilibrium. It is the critical mass. This is the point at which the network succeeds for the first time in generating as much benefit as the people participating in it want. C is not a stable equilibrium, however. Every point on the *U*-function between L and C reverts to L, failing. If the network fails to bring together enough people to generate enough benefits to go beyond C, then the network will fail. C is, therefore, the minimum extent of the network to function at all.

3. Point H is also an equilibrium. It is a stable equilibrium. The number of people at this point is so large that the network can no longer increase the benefits to such an extent that the expected benefits of the people participating are fulfilled. By point H, so many people have joined the network that they crowd each other out. Any additional person joining the network no longer contributes sufficiently to the benefits of the network. Up to point H, the additional benefit derived from the additional person is greater than expected by the users; from point H onwards, it is smaller. This means that point H represents the greatest extension of this network.

The equilibrium shifts from C to H with positive feedback. The positive feedback effect describes the process whereby a higher number of users increases the value of a network, which, in turn, motivates more people to join the network. It is a self-reinforcing process.

Equilibrium analysis seeks to analyze the dynamics of networks. Equilibria serve as a starting point for this. The interesting feature is that equilibrium is not so much what happens in a state of equilibrium as what happens when a network is not in equilibrium or when equilibrium is disturbed. So, what happens when a network is not on L, C, or H?

- If the number of people using the network lies between L and C, the network converges to L. It ceases to exist.
- Should the number of people using the network fall within points C and H, the network will converge to H. This means it will continue to expand until its maximum expansion, which is H.
- If the number of people using the network lies beyond point H, the network converges to H. As the benefit decreases beyond H, so does the number of people in the network. As a result, the network returns to its maximum extension, H.

This means that only L and H are stable equilibria. These are both possible outcomes of dynamic adaptation processes. Networks, therefore, tend to expand or contract as much as possible. This model suggests that *C is the point that networks want to reach as quickly as possible. Having reached C, networks must stay on the expansion path until they reach H, which is their maximum expansion.*

Of course, several caveats apply to the equilibrium model's suggestion. First, it only takes endogenous forces into account. It does not describe what happens when the network faces competition. In this case, users can exit the network for the competition even if the network has already crossed C. Second, it is doubtful whether every network has a point H. Maybe some networks are never saturated. In this case, the model cannot explain what happens after crossing C. Third, the model is heavily simplified. Remember that the efficacy of intermediation, e, is not factored in there.

2.9 Market Polarization

The equilibrium analysis would suggest that networks either fail, reverting to point L in Figure 2.7, or expand as much as possible, reaching point H. Such a tendency can give rise to market polarization in the network economy. This was something that Carl Shapiro and Hal Varian already recognized in their landmark book on network economics in 1998 (175):

In a situation where two or more companies are vying in a market with strong positive feedback, only one will emerge as the winner. Indeed, it is unlikely that the other or others will survive.

Markets where strong positive network and feedback effects come into play tend to polarize. This means the formation of monopolies. The equilibrium model outlined above shows that networks tend toward L or H. The same theory also states that only one will reach point H when several networks exist in the same market. This is because the maximum expansion of the network equals the maximum expansion of the market. All other networks active within the same market strive toward point L. This means they disappear. This is also known as the winner-take-all.

Example: Software Wars

In the 1980s and 1990s, the software race was still very much open. This applied to both operating systems and individual component software. Various word processing programs ran on the DOS and Windows operating systems, such as MSWord and Corel WordPerfect as word processing programs and Lotus 1-2-3 or Calculator as table processing programs. WordPerfect and Lotus 1-2-3 even appeared to be the market leaders by the end of the 1990s. Yet, as competition for H increased, the Microsoft programs were the first to achieve this equilibrium, and the competitors fell behind. Most of them left the market.

Markets with potential polarization tendencies are also referred to as tippy. A market is tippy when only one of several competitors can achieve critical mass and, therefore, prevail. The word comes from the

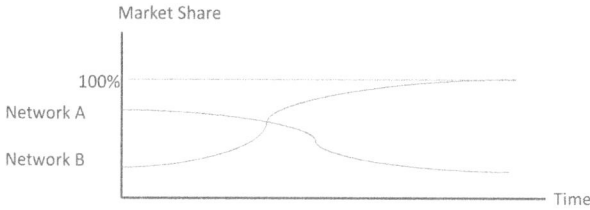

Figure 2.8 Tippy markets (own illustration)

verb to tip. This equilibrium theory states that these markets tip when one network establishes itself as dominant and then gradually squeezes the others out of the market.

Figure 2.8 shows an example of a tippy market. Two networks, networks A and B, compete in the same market. They aim to maximize their market share, that is, to expand as much as possible. The graph shows the changes in their respective market share over time. The market share they hold at the beginning is less critical. What is important is how their market shares develop. Network A does not manage to move from point C to H. This being the case, the market share falls, and the rate of change of the loss accelerates until a turning point is encountered, from which point it slows down again. This progression stems from the benefit function's concavity up and down. Network B successfully capitalizes on network effects and positive feedback and moves from C to H. The change rate of the market shares can also be traced back to the concavity of the benefit curve. Eventually, it reached 100 percent market share.

The respective turning points are important in this figure. Suppose network B successfully significantly increases the rate of change of its market shares. In that case, if it succeeds in deploying the concavity up of the benefit function, then the market will tip in its favor. This same tipping is felt by network A, in reverse. Economic theory suggests that the polarization trend is irreversible when both networks in this market have reached their respective turning points or tipping points. One network will endeavor to achieve a market share of 100 percent, and the other will probably be eliminated. The winner takes it all.

In practice, it is impossible to clearly capture such benefit functions and functions of the change rates of market shares to the extent envisaged by economic theory. A different typology has been established instead. It is a rule of thumb for predicting which markets are fairly tippy: *Markets with lock-in tend to be more tippy than those without, and markets with single-homing tend to be more tippy than those with multihoming.*

The *lock-in effect* makes people in one network unwilling to swap it for another. This is because every switch leads to particular transaction costs, that is, switching costs. Switching is only beneficial if the new benefits created by switching are greater than or equal to switching costs. Networks that understand how to increase the switching costs for their members implement a lock-in effect. For example, if an online dating platform only accepts cancellations by letter or fax, it increases the switching costs for its members. In doing so, a lock-in is implemented.

Single-homing refers to when a network user uses the network exclusively, meaning they only conduct their network activities in a single network. *Multihoming* applies when a network user conducts their activities across several parallel networks. For example, the person who gets their telephone, TV, and data services from the same network is single-homing; the person using Twitter, TikTok, and XING as social media simultaneously is multihoming.

Economic theory suggests that direct network effects are more prevalent in single-homing and lock-in. Such effects result in more robust positive feedback and, consequently, more pronounced network effects. This means:

- Lock-in effects, single-homing, indirect network effects, and economies of scale are more likely to generate market polarization.
- Multihoming, crowding-out effects, platform differentiation, and direct network effects are more likely to hold back market polarization.

2.10 Critical Assessment

Network effects are the heart of network economics. These effects are, in principle, easy to describe. Nevertheless, it is a challenge to systematize and model them. Economic theory addresses network effects using standard equilibrium models adapted to platforms. These models have strengths and weaknesses. The strengths of the equilibrium models include:

- They make thinking more systematic by analyzing cause-and-effect mechanisms. Abstract benefit functions are formulated and balanced against each other. As a result, influencing factors and their relationships can be studied in more detail.
- It is possible to visualize changes using models. On the one hand, this is done by changing and comparing the specific model forms. On the other hand, the effects of changes to individual elements on the overall result can be analyzed.
- Equilibrium models examine the dynamics of network effects. This is because they focus on the twofold question of how networks reach which equilibria.
- This focus means that the models can explain some internal interrelationships and the real implications of networks and network effects.

But equilibrium models also have weaknesses:

- Each network functions differently. Therefore, the respective dynamics of the network effects are specific to each network. Whether they are at all similar in phenotype is unclear.

- It is impossible to determine the exact points C and H, or at least from an ex-ante perspective. Until now, no equilibrium model has successfully determined a network's critical mass and maximum possible extent. This is because the limits of the network itself change.
- There are also many practical examples of networks that go beyond a presumed C but do not reach H without falling back to L. Such networks settle between C and H and can be useful for certain people. These include email providers, for example. These compete against each other and exist side by side without reaching H. This also makes it unclear whether

and how tippyness can be determined—at least from an ex-ante
perspective.

- These are reasons why equilibrium models have a hard time
  explaining networks. The chicken and egg problem, lock-in, and
  homing demonstrate that network effects alone do not yield
  results or equilibria in practice. The network provider generally does more than implement network effects. The network
  business model is implemented by establishing and putting in
  place governance. It is anything but rule-based in its implementation. Instead, it is a process of discovery involving constant
  experimentation and the network effects being reorganized and
  put together in new ways.

Regarding tippyness, it is not trivial to determine a market.
Equilibrium models lead to deliberations about market polarization.
This involves establishing that a market can tip, that is, a network can
establish a monopoly. While this follows from theory, the fundamental
question of what this *market* actually is or where its boundaries are to
be drawn cannot be answered by theory. So-called market definitions
constitute a much-discussed problem. Economic theory cannot fully
explain what is part of one market and what is already part of another.
After all, the definition of a market is always a conscious decision made
by the person defining it. Different results are achieved depending on
how this decision is made. An example can be used to illustrate this:

Google is often criticized for having a quasi-monopoly on the
internet search engine market. This is a very problematic allegation in
economic terms. It may be intuitively true, but it is still challenging to
substantiate it economically.

The first problem is that besides Google, other search engines such
as Yahoo, Bing, DuckDuckGo, or Ecosia exist. These engines seem to
operate without falling out of the market. So, all of them, including
Google, are between C and H.

The second problem is that Google does not sell search services but
makes them free. The users do not pay to use the search engine. Google
relies on them as suppliers of information. Those who use Google agree
that Google will browse users' search behavior to provide information to

the *other market side*. The other market side comprises companies that need information from Google to tailor their advertising. The Google search engine does not earn money by collecting information but by channeling advertising. As a result, there is no market for internet search engines; it is an advertising market in which Google is merely a channel.

The third problem is that if Google is a channel in the advertising market, it competes for advertising budgets with all other channels: TV stations, newspapers, and so on, Even if the relevant market is to be narrowed down to the internet, Google still competes with all websites offering advertising space. It competes primarily with Facebook and Twitter. Even if we take an even narrower definition of the advertising market to search engines alone, there is still a lot of competition. There are direct competitors such as Yahoo or Microsoft's Bing, alongside specialized search engines for books, auctions, classified ads, restaurants, travel, and dating.

The fourth problem: This market is developing rapidly. It is anything but a given that Google will remain uncontested, no matter its market segment. It is not just that the competition is a click away; the stronger Google is, the more investment is made in disruptive innovation.

Summary

- A network creates benefits by connecting people.
- Benefit involves the individual-subjective improvement of each person and the entire network compared to a situation without a network.
- Direct networks emerge when the benefits of the individuals and the group increase within a group of people who use a network when additional people join the group. In turn, this makes joining and the network itself more attractive to others.
- Indirect network effects emerge when the expansion of one group of people improves the situation of another group in the same network. The increase in the size of one group makes joining and, consequently, the network more attractive for the other group.

- Economic theory uses benefit functions to model the benefits of the network. It draws on the *laws* of computer science, Sarnoff, Metcalfe, Reed, and deceleration.
- A nuanced network model combines the people's benefit function using the network—demand—with the network provider's (supply) benefit function to determine equilibria.
- The nuanced benefit function of the people using the network considers the varying benefits of the network's start-up phase, expansion, and consolidation until it is as large as possible.
- The network's sponsor nuanced benefit function considers the various benefits generated by the provider. In the beginning, the provider itself is responsible for generating the benefits. As time passes, they pass on the task since demand generates benefits in the network itself through network effects.
- The equilibrium theory implies that networks must exceed a critical mass of people since, otherwise, they will not be able to survive.
- The equilibrium theory also suggests that networks exceeding their critical mass achieve maximum possible expansion, meaning their market share strives toward 100 percent. This leads to polarization tendencies in the network economy.
- Practice does not confirm these considerations. Experience with networks suggests that they are embedded in dynamic discovery and adaptation processes. Solutions to chicken and egg problems, homing, and lock-in are just a few examples of the network provider's active role during all network phases.
- Network effects cannot explain everything that happens in a network.
- Outlook: the next chapter focuses on pricing in networks.

Review Questions

First Series: Which Statements Are Correct? Which Are Not?

1. Positive network effects always occur.

2. The number of connections that a network can create between its members provides a good indication of the benefits that the network brings.

3. Direct network effects occur when one group of people becomes more attractive when another group becomes bigger.

4. If a network grows too big, crowding-out effects appear.

5. If a person conducts all their purchases through one platform, this is known as multihoming.

6. The equilibrium model states that H and L are stable equilibria.

7. The critical mass corresponds to the sum of functions a network must fulfill before people use it.

8. There are still no practical solutions to the chicken and egg problem.

9. Economic theory suggests that networks gravitate toward H-equilibrium. This results in polarization tendencies in markets with networks.

10. Lock-in effects are particularly prevalent when switching costs are high.

Second Series: Solve the Following Challenges

1. Explain positive direct network effects, taking Adobe Acrobat as an example, specifically the PDF format

2. Explain negative direct network effects, taking eBay as an example.

3. Explain positive indirect network effects, taking the example of Blu-Ray.

4. Explain the positive feedback, taking Uber as an example (search the web for *Uber's business model on a napkin*).

5. Explain the tendency toward polarization in network markets by referring to the developments of Myspace and Facebook.

6. Challenge the assumed polarization tendency by addressing multihoming based on the example of Facebook.

7. A company pursues the business model of caring for senior citizens in their homes. The company plans on transforming the

business model into a platform. How can it solve the chicken and egg problem?

8. Why does Sarnoff's Law better explain the business model of public broadcasters, and Metcalfe's Law better explain the business model of private broadcasters?

9. Identify three examples of markets with networks where the polarization tendency has not occurred.

10. Describe the network effects in the following examples: YouTube, Yelp, Amazon Kindle.

Third Series: Respond to the Following Questions and Solve the Mini-Case Studies

1. How did BlaBlaCar reach critical mass?

2. Which markets are Facebook, Twitter, and Instagram active in?

3. Cite an example that clearly illustrates how different market definitions result in completely different conclusions regarding polarization tendencies.

4. Which role does substitutability play in the network economy?

5. Which influencing factors impact the form and position of the analytical benefit function, the demand?

6. Which influencing factors impact the form and position of the analytical supply function of supply?

7. Discuss whether the following equilibrium is possible; if it is, cite an example. The equilibrium is $C = H$.

8. What are platform wars? How do they relate to the equilibrium model presented here?

9. How are platform wars linked to polarization tendencies?

10. What non-monetary lock-in effects exist for membership in an association?

Commented Bibliography

*   Belleflamme, P. and M. Peitz. 2018. *The Economics of Platforms.* Cambridge University Press.

- o One of the latest introductions to the economic theory of networks. Incorporates many examples.
- Eisenmann, T., G. Parker, and M.W. Van Alstyne. 2006. Strategies for Two-Sided Markets. *Harvard Business Review* 84(10): 92.
  - o General summary of network theory. Classic article that can cater to both theoretical and practical requirements.
- Manne, G.A. and J.D. Wright. 2011. "Google and the Limits of Antitrust: The Case Against the Antitrust Case Against Google." *Harvard Journal of Law and Public Policy* 34: 171.
  - o Careful and differentiated explanation of polarization effects, including when they can and cannot occur. The article also presents a practical discussion of the criteria for defining the market.
- Rysman, M. 2009. "The Economics of Two-Sided Markets." *Journal of Economic Perspectives* 23(3): 125–143.
  - o This classic article deals with the economic theory of two-sided markets.
- Shapiro, C., S. Carl, and H.R. Varian. 1998. *Information Rules: A Strategic Guide to the Network Economy.* Harvard Business Press.
  - o Classic textbook as an introduction to network effects. Balances theoretical and practical aspects.

CHAPTER 3

Pricing

This chapter covers how prices are set in networks. More specifically, it deals with the price, even better: prices the network's sponsor sets for people to join and use the network. Network pricing depends on how much one benefits from the network. But it also has a different component. The network's sponsor aims to increase reach. Both elements are traded against one another, resulting in a multi-layered pricing system. This chapter outlines and compares various pricing models. It pays attention to phenomena typical for digital networks, such as subsidization, differentiation, and dynamization of prices. After reading this chapter, you will be able to:

- Section 3.1: explain the economic aspects of prices and pricing.
- Section 3.2: calculate the added value in networks.
- Section 3.3: determine prices in equilibrium models.
- Section 3.4: ascertain the effect of elasticity in pricing.
- Section 3.5: set prices for a network business model.
- Section 3.6: refine pricing by incorporating network effects into it.
- Section 3.7: expand pricing by applying an analytical model.
- Section 3.8: differentiate prices.
- Section 3.9: gain an overview of various considerations for pricing in practice.
- Section 3.10: critically assess the contents of this chapter.

3.1 Price

Chapter 2 illustrated the benefits of a network as a function of the connections made within it. A network's capacity to combine these connections with a price mechanism creates value. The economic value creation of a network corresponds to the sum of the prices paid by these individuals or groups for these connections and the transactions resulting from them.

Economic value creation is the benefit level of an economic activity as expressed in monetary units by prices. Prices express the individual-subjective benefit into an objectifiable unit. Prices say how much people value something. As usual, by people, all types of agents are meant, humans and companies.

Before discussing a platform's price mechanism, we need to understand the concept of price and how it differs from costs and benefits.

Cost, Benefit, and Price

Let us use a pipeline business model, such as a car manufacturer, as an example. Assume it costs 10,000 USD to make a car. From the supplier's point of view, putting a car together consumes 10,000 USD worth of resources, such as labor and material. From the supplier's point of view, it cost them 10,000 USD to make and offer a car for sale.

Let us switch the perspective to demand or potential demand, assuming that the manufacturer sells directly to people. To a person who does not drive a car, the vehicle creates no benefit and is therefore worthless. Someone else might be willing to pay up to 30,000 dollars for the vehicle. According to this person's individual-subjective calculation, the car generates a benefit. The benefit corresponds to this person's willingness to pay. To that person's liking, the car is worth 30,000 dollars.

The challenge lies here: Both costs and willingness to pay tend to be private knowledge. It is not shared or communicated. If the buyer does not tell the seller their willingness to pay, the seller can hardly gauge it. Inversely, the seller never discloses how much it costs to make a car. The way these two agents find each other is by communicating via prices. Technically, they do so by using bid- and ask-prices. The term *bid* refers to the highest price a buyer will pay to buy a specified number of shares of a stock at any given time. The term *ask* refers to the lowest price at which a seller will sell the stock. These prices become public knowledge the moment they are communicated between agents. After some communication, the bid will equal the ask, and a clearing price is found. For that price, the car is sold and bought.

Let us say the buyer and seller both settled for 20,000 dollars. In the supplier's or seller's eyes, this is 10,000 dollars more than it cost him to produce the car, which is a profit. In the buyer's eyes, the car generates a benefit of 30,000 dollars, but they only pay 20,000 for it. This is a gain in welfare.

But what about the person whose willingness to pay for the car is zero? That person did not participate in this exchange. Their welfare was equal to before, so they did not see an increase but did not lose any money.

The following example can get a little more complicated: the Churchill Solitaire app, a network business model, and an online game. Remember OPEX? For the network sponsor and the app programmer, there is no cost associated with the individual game. Whether one person or 10 million people play the game, the game as such costs zero dollars. However, the person playing the game will have to pay for it. Depending on the location, the person playing pays two USD per game or subscribes to the app. Anyone prepared to pay two dollars or more for a game will do so. The price reveals some of the willingness to pay. Then there is also a free version of the app. However, the person accessing it is confronted with in-app ads and upselling. By the way, this app's proceeds will be donated to social causes.

What do these examples highlight?

- The network's sponsor bears the CAPEX (Capital costs, see chapter 1) and OPEX (operational costs, see chapter 1). Even if the costs are essential, they are only important from the sponsor's perspective. The value of the connection, intermediation, and transaction has nothing to do with these costs. It is not even possible to derive prices from the costs. The value of something is the result of communication between buyer and seller.

- People who are using or thinking of joining the network determine for themselves how much they are willing to pay. This is an individual-subjective determination. Each agent has their own idea of how beneficial a network is and, therefore, an individual's willingness to pay. This determination is heavily dependent on context.

- Cost and willingness to pay are private information. Often, willingness to pay does not even exist explicitly. They are partially revealed when supply and demand negotiate prices. The price paid is the result of negotiations in a market process. Often, these negotiations are not explicit and occur only at an aggregated level. But they do occur, for prices communicate to suppliers what consumers want, and prices communicate to consumers what suppliers can make. At a social level, prices are feedback mechanisms. Sometimes, prices are customized to match the personal preferences of consumers and producers. This is known as *price differentiation*.

In summary, like most economic phenomena, pricing is often a discovery process: Suppliers discover how those enquiring measure value, and consumers discover the cost structure of those supplying. This takes place in an infinite number of interactions, reactions, and counter-reactions. The less regulated, more decentralized, and spontaneous the process, the more beneficial it is for the people involved.

Economists assert that prices have several functions in a market economy:

- Signal/information function: The price says a great deal about a commodity's scarcity. Price changes reveal shifts in the relationship between demand and availability or supply. When the price rises, it can be assumed that a commodity is becoming increasingly scarce. Price changes also signal that the respective cost and value perceptions are changing. The easier or more dynamic prices can adapt, the better they fulfill this function.

- Steering/allocation function: By its very nature, the price steers the factors of production in the direction of the profits to be achieved. In other words, the price steers supply and, consequently, the use of production factors toward the markets where demand is more willing to pay. Prices set incentives. Suppliers produce commodities that people are willing to pay for. The willingness to pay represents an approximation of the value estimate of the enquirers.

- Balancing/planning coordination function: Prices balance supply and demand by reflecting the outcome of their negotiations. This makes prices efficient planning instruments because they facilitate comparability at a glance. This more straightforward comparability reduces transaction costs and simplifies the coordination of demand and supply and the planning process.

- Readout function: Regarding demand, prices ensure that only those genuinely interested in the commodity buy it. So, prices minimize waste. Regarding supply, prices indicate whether commodities are worth paying for or not. Commodities that are worth it lead to a benefit surplus for both demand and supply. The company providing such a commodity can offset its costs with the price and generate a profit. The price mechanism implements something like a traffic light system for companies. When the price is adequate so that costs are covered, and a profit is made, the traffic light is green; there is a benefit for supply and demand. If costs cannot be offset by the price, that is, the company makes a loss, and the traffic light is amber. It is not possible to fulfill the value expectations of demand. Should the price be permanently below the costs, the company goes bust. The traffic light is red because the supply has not created benefits. This company, or at the very least the product, drops out of the market processes.

3.2 Value Creation

Price is one element of economic value creation, technically defined as the difference between output and input or revenues and costs. In its most rudimentary form, one can write an equation for the value add or the value creation as such:

Value Added = Output – Input = Revenues – Costs

Revenue is the income generated by an economic activity. It is the product of all the units sold times the price at which the unit was sold. In the case of platforms, depending on the platform's capitalization, it is the number of connections or transactions times the price per connection or transaction.

Of course, this equation cannot be more than an approximation. By starting with the revenues, the formula leaves out the willingness to pay. However, the difference between it and the price paid is the consumer's welfare, an essential factor in any economic consideration. On the other hand, the formula imputes all costs, CAPEX and OPEX. Despite these problems, the equation still gives a good idea of economic value creation: The welfare created by the output of an economic activity when all its inputs are discounted.

Let us see how economic value is created by a platform in an example:

A Platform for the Global Supply Chain

Trust Square, a co-working space, is an example of a non-digital network that aims to establish a consulting platform for global companies' supply chains. This platform is based on peer consulting, that is, participants provide each other with advice. Supply chain managers from various companies gather to advise each other every two months.

Trust Square is a co-working space without substantive connection or expertise regarding the supply chain. And that is how it should stay because Trust Square is committed to remaining a network operator, not a user. As a network sponsor, it connects three market sides: A content team puts together the session content, prepares the sessions, follows up, and moderates them. The supply chain managers attending the sessions pose questions and advise each other. Donors pay for the platform.

Trust Square incurs costs totaling 25,000 dollars and is financed by sponsorship contributions of 30,000 dollars. This means that the value created by this network is 5,000 dollars. However, this does not say anything about what the people who use the network see as added value. What does the individual calculation of these three market sides look like?

- The content team pays a price in kind. It is responsible for organizing the sessions and for the content. This goes hand in hand with a great deal of preparation and responsibility. The individual members of the team accept this, however, because the benefits of the platform are high in their individual and subjective assessments: they can raise their profile, they can set standards in the supply chain, connect with managers, and learn a great deal. These efforts are irrelevant to the economic value calculation because they yield no dollar price.
- The participants do not pay any monetary price. They do, however, put in the time to come to the meetings, disclose information about themselves, and pass on their knowledge in peer consulting. The fact that they learn more than they give and can save on expensive consultants is their benefit calculation. They participate in the platform if this individually and subjectively assessed benefit exceeds the so-called opportunity cost of participating. Again, these efforts are irrelevant to the economic value calculation because they yield no dollar price.

- Donors pay a price, their donation, in the form of money to Trust Square, which then pays its costs and makes a profit from the sum of donations. Of course, no money flows to the other market sides. The donors themselves are software companies, financial institutions, or transportation companies looking for information from supply chain managers and direct access to them. If their benefit is higher than or equal to their donations in the dollars. Otherwise, they would not donate to the network. As the donation is in money, it counts as the revenue for the equation of value added.

  One important feature of many platforms springs to mind in this example: Two sides do not pay dollar amounts to participate. One side pays for all, which effectively is a subsidy. We will see that subsidizing some groups by others plays an important role in networks. And we also see that not all costs and benefits are captured by the equation.

  By the way, Trust Square could further develop its pricing mechanism by differentiating between the willingness to pay off the different donors, for example, by creating categories such as gold, silver, and bronze. Trust Square can also set customized prices depending on how negotiations proceed.

In this example, we saw how a platform's sponsor creates value by intermediating. Trust Square decided to capitalize on the connection instead of the transaction. At least one group, the donors, pays to access the network and its potential connections. In this example, whether and how much they transact via the platform does not influence the price. However, the price for connection is sufficiently high to generate a profit for the platform. The price is also enough to create at least so much benefit to make the other sides want to participate. The content team and participants are being subsidized because their platform use is free.

While no one will doubt that the platform is creating value, even economic value for all sides, only the dollar amount can be computed because only one side pays a price in dollars. Therefore, as explained before, the network's value added is 5,000 dollars.

Prices and value creation are thus interrelated. The price mechanism allows economic activity to be realized and measured as value creation. The joint creation of value in exchange processes is achieved with prices. In theory, value added is the product of units sold and the price per unit. However, as the example shows, pricing is less straightforward on platforms.

Let us systematize this discussion by, once again, using economic theory to elucidate. We will look at pricing in traditional markets, that is, markets in equilibrium, and then expand the perspective to networks.

3.3 Price in Equilibrium Markets

The market in equilibrium is a powerful tool in economic theory. It helps us understand how prices are made. The usual caution applies here. Equilibrium models are, well, models. They are not a description of reality but an explanatory tool. With this tool, we analyze and understand pricing in an abstract form. Implementing pricing is another story. While practitioners can or should use the model as a point of departure, it will need many adaptations to singular contexts.

In Chapter 2, we already dealt with economic equilibrium. We will discuss it more in-depth now and need, first, to get to know the model of a market in equilibrium in more detail:

- There are two parameters or variables: price and quantity.
- There are two types of agents: demand and supply.
- The willingness of suppliers and consumers to transact in a market is expressed in price-quantity combinations. This means that all value concepts of demand and all cost structures of supply are translated into combinations of prices and quantities. These are known as the demand and supply functions, respectively.
- The general willingness of supply to transact and the course of the supply function can be summarized as such: the higher the price, the greater the quantity supplied.

- The general willingness of demand to transact and the course of the demand function can be summarized as such: the lower the price, the greater the quantity demanded.
- The demand function and the supply function equal each other at the equilibrium. Graphically, the demand curve intersects the supply curve.
- The results of this equilibrium are the equilibrium price and the equilibrium quantity. The equilibrium price is the only price where the willingness of consumers and producers agree—that is, where the amount of the product consumers want to buy (quantity demanded) equals the amount producers want to sell (quantity supplied).
- In this model, nothing other than the two functions, or curves, plays a role. This is called the *ceteris paribus* assumption, all else being equal.

Figure 3.1 shows how the market in equilibrium works. The parameters, or variables, are the axes. The price is on the ordinate (y-axis), and the quantity is on the abscissa (x-axis). Supply and Demand are the graph's lines (economists say curves). Note that they are

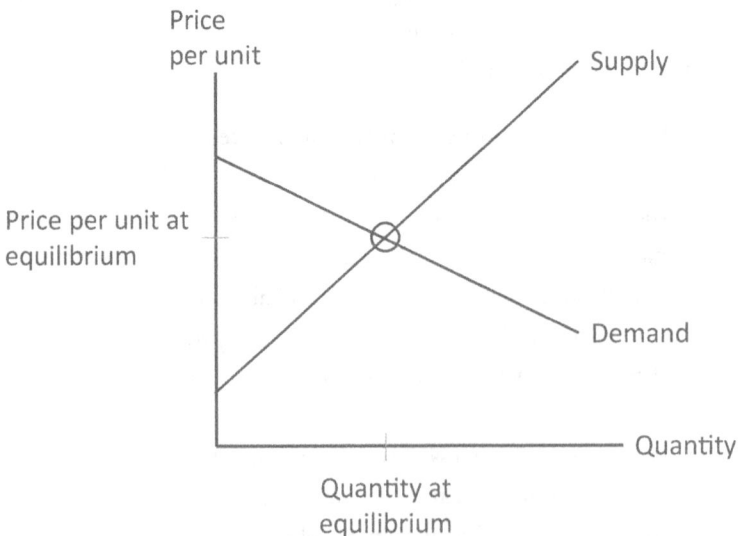

Figure 3.1 Model of the equilibrium market (own illustration)

independent of each other. The slope of the demand curve is negative, indicating that the falling price increases the demanded quantity. The slope of the supply curve is positive because the higher price leads to an increase in the quantity supplied.

There is one point and only one where the demand and supply functions intersect. That point is marked with a circle in the graph. This exact point is the market's equilibrium. When both curves meet, there is one price, the unit price at equilibrium, and one quantity, the quantity at equilibrium. Economic theory assumes that the respective benefits of supply and demand, as far as they can be measured or approximated, are maximized in equilibrium.

Now, let us use the model to see how changes in supply and demand influence the equilibrium. Many things influence supply and demand, changing their functions. Graphically, their curves rotate and shift. If the curves are displaced, the equilibrium changes its position, too. With that, new combinations of unit prices and quantities clearing the market emerge. This is the value added of this model: One can picture what happens to equilibrium when supply and demand change.

Figure 3.2 shows an equilibrium market with a shift in the supply line (or curve). This is a random example to illustrate the changes

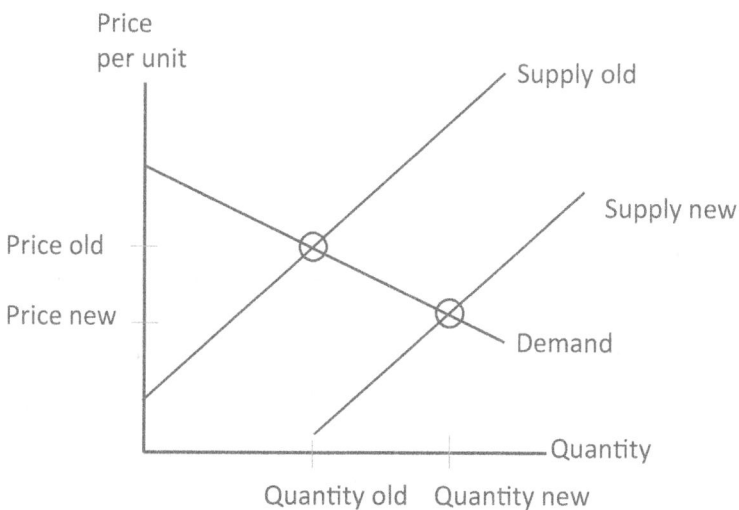

Figure 3.2 Equilibrium market after shift in supply (own illustration)

in equilibrium. In this case, there has been a rightward shift in the supply curve. This typically occurs when production costs are reduced, and this reduction is passed on to the market. The production of tablets is an example of this. With increasing reductions in the cost of production factors and the scaling of the corresponding technology, it is possible to pass these advantages on to the market. This is accepted by demand; as the price falls, it expands the quantity demanded.

A lower equilibrium price and a larger equilibrium quantity than the old one characterize the new equilibrium. Expressed as a cause-and-effect relationship: Reducing the production price leads to a rightward shift in the supply curve. This results in a shift of the equilibrium and, consequently, to a new point with a lower equilibrium price and a larger equilibrium quantity.

The shift in equilibrium in this model depends, on the one hand, upon the respective change in the willingness of supply and demand. The effect differs depending on how much the curves shift or rotate. On the other hand, this shift also depends on the shape of the supply and demand function. Expressed in graphical terms, the shift depends on the slope of the lines. The shift of a steep line produces a different effect than a relatively flat line. The inclination of the lines or slope is called elasticity.

3.4 Elasticity

Did you notice that the slopes of the demand and supply curves are not the same? Of course not, since one is positive and the other negative. But even their absolute numbers are different. There is an economic meaning to it. A steep or flat slope shows the elasticity of a curve.

Elasticity refers to the responsiveness of one variable to changes in another variable. It is commonly used to assess how the quantity demanded or supplied of a good or service responds to changes in price, income, or other factors. Price elasticity of demand, for example, indicates how much the quantity demanded of a good changes when its price changes. If a small change in price leads to a significant change in quantity demanded, the good is considered elastic. Conversely, the good is inelastic if the quantity demanded changes little with price fluctuations.

Similarly, price elasticity of supply measures how much the quantity supplied of good changes in response to a price change. Supply is elastic if producers can increase output significantly when prices rise. If they cannot adjust production easily, supply is inelastic. Just as a reminder: There are several types of elasticity, not just price elasticity of demand and supply. To understand networks, we focus on the price elasticity of demand.

Figure 3.3 shows two markets in equilibrium. The equilibrium point is marked with a circle. The parameters or variables are the same as those viewed above, as well as the price per unit and quantity. There is a supply line or curve. The parameters and the supply are identical in both graphs of the figure. The graphs also feature a demand line or curve, but they differ. The course of the demand curve on the left is flat, and the one on the right is steep.

This difference in slope has consequences. The demand curve on the left, with its small slope and flat course, is price-elastic. The one on the right, with its high slope and steep course, is price-inelastic.

When the demand for a good or service is price-elastic, a small change in price results in a significant change in the quantity demanded. Goods with elastic demand usually have readily available substitutes, are not necessities, or consume a large portion of the consumer's budget. For example, luxury items or nonessential goods often have elastic demand. If the price of a luxury car increases significantly, the quantity

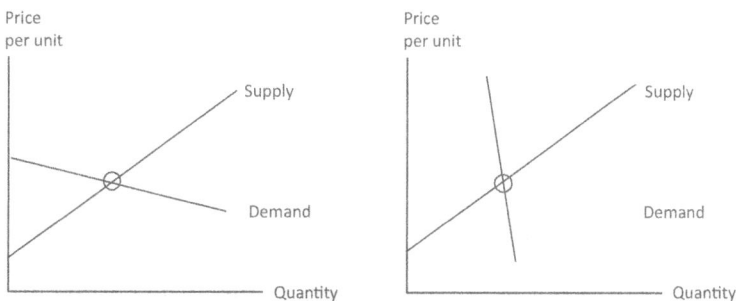

Figure 3.3 Price elasticity of demand (own illustration)

demanded will likely drop substantially because consumers can either forego the purchase or choose a different brand.

Conversely, when the demand for a good or service is price-inelastic, changes in price have little effect on the quantity demanded. Goods with inelastic demand typically lack close substitutes, are necessities, or represent a small portion of the consumer's budget. For instance, essential medications, basic food items, and gasoline tend to have inelastic demand. Even if prices rise, consumers will continue to purchase almost the same quantity because they need these items regardless of price changes.

So, the curve's steepness becomes more meaningful when it changes position. Depending on its elasticity, a shift in the demand curve significantly changes a market's equilibrium. Figure 3.4 shows this.

Figure 3.4 shows the effects of different price elasticities of demand. In principle, it replicates Figure 3.3. There are two graphs, one on the left with a price-elastic demand and one on the right with a price-inelastic demand. We compare the effect of the same increase in price on the two differently sloped demand lines. We begin with the equilibrium marked with a circle. The first set of equilibria that interests us is the lower and rightward circles in the respective graphs. Now, for some reason, the supply curve shifts to the left, indicating some disruption in the supply chain, and the price goes up. The arrow outside the graph symbolizes this to the left of the left axis.

This increase is not the same in two graphs, left and right. This increase leads to a second set of equilibria, both more to the left and

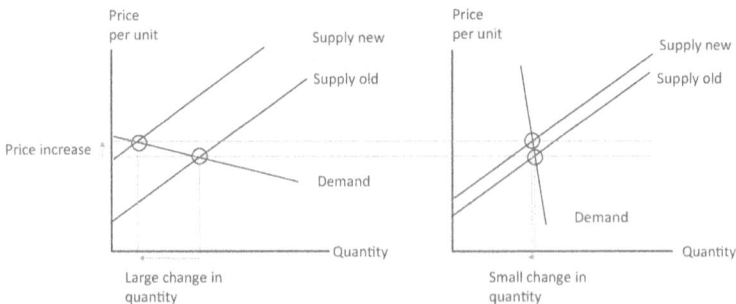

Figure 3.4 Effects of different price elasticities of demand (own illustration)

upward from the first set. In the left graph, the increase in price leads to a large change in quantity. Because of the price-inelastic demand curve, demand exists in this market, looking for substitutes. The effect is that the quantity reduction is overproportionate to the increase in price per unit. In the right graph, the effect is different. The price-inelastic demand cannot substitute. It mostly absorbs the price change. True: There is a reduction in the quantity demanded. But this reduction is so small that it is barely shown on the graph. It is underproportionate to the increase in price per unit. This leaves us with two insights:

- When the price elasticity of demand is elastic or flat, demand can substitute the product or service. Changes in price lead to an overproportionate change in demanded quantity.
- When the price elasticity of demand is inelastic or steep, demand cannot substitute the product or service. Changes in price lead to an underproportionate change in demanded quantity.

This direct price elasticity in demand can be calculated as:

$$e = \Delta Q \,[in\, \%] \,/\, \Delta p \,[in\, \%]$$

This formula uses e for the elasticity coefficient; do not confuse it with e for the efficacy of the intermediation in a network. The Greek delta Δ denotes a change, specifically the change in quantity Q over the change in price P. Here, the changes are calculated in percent. For example, if the price changes by 10 percent and the quantity demanded changes by 20 percent, the price elasticity of this demand is $e = 2$.

What does $e = 2$ mean? If $e = 1$, the changes in price and quantity are the same. If the price per unit falls by 5 percent, the demanded quantity increases by 5 percent. If $e > 1$, the quantity demanded is adjusted overproportionately to the changes in price, as in the example just given, $e = 2$. This price elasticity of demand is elastic. If $e < 1$, the quantity demanded is adjusted underproportionately to the change in price. This is a price-inelastic demand.

As mentioned earlier, the price elasticity of demand for a good or service depends on the possibility of substitution. This statement means that the degree to which consumers can find and switch to alternative products affects how sensitive the quantity demanded is to changes in price.

- When readily available substitutes exist for a good or service, the demand for that good or service tends to be more price-elastic. This is because if the price of the good increases, consumers can easily switch to a substitute that offers a similar benefit at a lower price.
- On the other hand, when few or no close substitutes are available, the demand for the good or service is more price-inelastic. In such cases, consumers have limited alternatives even if the price increases and must continue purchasing the good despite the higher cost.

But substitution is neither a given nor absolute. Suppliers can try to influence the substitution. Let us review this in an example.

Unique Tortilla Chips

A food processor, a pipeline business model, produces two types of tortilla chips. The first type has a well-recognized brand and a unique form. The second type is a tortilla chip, as many others are in the market.

Market research reveals that for the first type of chip, a price change of 10 percent results in a change in the demanded quantity of 5 percent. The same price change for the second type results in a change in the demanded quantity of 15 percent. The question is now, what can this producer do with such information?

For the first type of chip, $e = (5/10) = 0.5$. Since $e < 1$, this demand is inelastic to price. In this case, a price increase results in higher revenues and profits if costs are kept the same. While less quantity is sold, the price increase more than compensates for this decrease. The excellent positioning of the chip in the market is such that consumers are prepared to pay a higher price. The reduction of demanded quantity is disproportionately low because customers do not substitute this chip well.

For the second type of chip, $e = (15/10) = 1.5$. Since $e > 1$, this demand is elastic to price. For this type of chip, the producer should lower the price. With the lower price, the demanded quantity increases overproportionately. The price reduction, therefore, results in more revenues and, if costs are kept the same, higher profits. When it comes to price-elastic goods and services, consumers substitute. A price reduction is greeted by consumers, who substitute into this market and product, expanding the demanded quantity.

What did we learn here?

- For a price-elastic demand, reducing prices increases the quantity and revenues, and the profit in costs is kept constant.
- For a price-inelastic demand, rising prices decreases the quantity but increases the revenues, and the profit in costs is kept constant.

Be aware: As with everything economic, the price elasticity of demand depends on the respective situation. For example, the demand for bottled water in a supermarket is elastic in terms of price. Not only can most waters be substituted for one another at will, but they are also available side by side on the shelves. The transaction costs for substitution are especially low in supermarkets.

In a restaurant, the situation is entirely different. Most restaurants only carry a few or only one type of bottled water. You could still replace water with cola or beer, but it is no longer so easy to substitute. Therefore, the demand for bottled water in restaurants is more price-inelastic than in supermarkets. On budget airlines, it is even less elastic. Anyone wishing to drink bottled water during the flight must order what is in stock on the plane. The price set by the airline must also be paid. There is almost no substitution during the flight, except for similarly priced goods. It is undoubtedly possible to stock up on water beforehand, but this is already too high a transaction cost for many people. In any case, the more price-inelastic, the higher the price.

With this, we completed the groundwork for the next step. We now know how to think of prices as the outcomes of market equilibria, which depend on the price elasticity of demand. However, our examples so far have been applied to markets in which demand and supply are directly met. How does this change when they deal with an intermediary, the platform's sponsor?

3.5 Naive Pricing in Two-Sided Markets

Naïve pricing transfers the findings of price formation in equilibrium markets to networks. To illustrate this, we explain this using a two-sided market. A two-sided market is a network that mediates between two groups of people. The network establishes connections between two groups, each wanting something from the other. The objective of the connections is to facilitate an exchange between the members of the respective groups. There is little or hardly any exchange within the groups.

Let us introduce a hypothetical example to guide us through the following steps. "HNDWK" is an online platform that connects handyworkers with households. It works like this:

- One side of the platform is the handyworkers. On this side, they form the demand for connections. The network supplies them with connections.
- The other side of the platform is the households. On this side, they form the demand for connections, and the network supplies them.
- Note how the platform's sponsor is the supply to both sides. They supply connections to the handyworkers and households.
- Whenever a transaction is made via the network, those involved remunerate the sponsor. For example, if a handyworker is matched to a household to repair a sink for 23 dollars per hour, the platform is remunerated.

- What interests us here is the remuneration of the platform's sponsor, not the price for repairing a sink. So, how does the platform set a price for intermediating the transaction?
- As a supplier to two-sided, the platform is faced with two different lines of demand: those of the handyworkers and those of households.

With *naive* pricing, the platform implements the equilibrium prices for each demand line.

Figure 3.5 shows this naïve pricing. It is called naïve because it follows the equilibrium logic. It finds equilibria in each market side and makes the equilibrium price for each side. In Figure 3.5, both sides of the platform are shown. On the left is the market side of households, and on the right are handyworkers. As mentioned before, the platform is the supply on both sides. In each market, there is an equilibrium marked with a circle.

The axes named price per unit show the price per intermediated transaction, and the axes named quantity show the number of intermediated transactions via the platform.

The equilibrium on the left graph yields the price Pa and the quantity Qa, and on the right, Pb and Qb. This means the platform will charge households with Pa and handyworkers with Pb—in dollars per transaction whenever a transaction succeeds. At these prices, the platform can intermediate Qa transactions with households and Qb transactions with handyworkers.

The total revenue TR of the platform is:

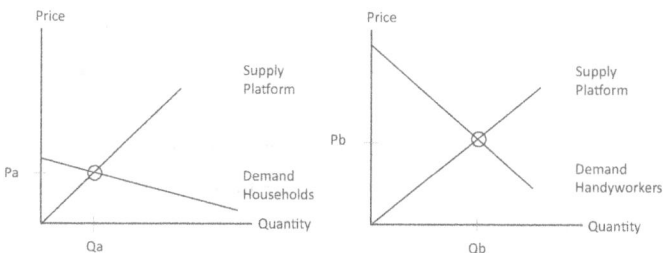

Figure 3.5 Naïve pricing in two-sided markets (own illustration)

$$TR = (Pa \bullet Qa) + (Pb \bullet Qb)$$

The economic value added by the platform is the difference between its total revenues TR and costs TC:

$$Value\ added = TR - TC = (Pa \bullet Qa) + (Pb \bullet Qb) - TC$$

However, there are two problems with naïve pricing. The first concerns economic theory. This type of pricing fails to include network effects. The second concerns managerial desiderata: The value added generated with this kind of pricing is much lower than it could be if network effects were considered and included.

There is no question: Based on the equilibrium model, the respective equilibria maximize the value creation of this platform if the markets are each treated separately. The missing factor here, however, is the network effects, as explained in the previous chapter. The main feature of the platform is to create network effects. They have been left out of the model.

We can assume that this platform will become more attractive for households if more handyworkers can be found on it. Similarly, the platform will be more attractive to handyworkers if many households can be found on it. What does it mean to become more attractive? It means there will be more people on the platform and more transactions, increasing Qa and Qb.

In addition, you have certainly noticed that the slope of both demand lines differed. Households and handyworkers have different possibilities of substituting the platform's intermediation. The difference in slope hints that elasticity will play a role in a better pricing model in two-sided business models.

Where does this leave us? Naïve pricing means looking for market-specific equilibria in the sides intermediated by a platform. However, naïve pricing fails to include network effects and does not pay sufficient attention to the price elasticity of each demand of the side being connected by the platform. Therefore, we need a better pricing model for network business models.

3.6 Pricing With Network Effects

In pricing with network effects, the platform's sponsor will seek the optimum pricing for the whole network, not only for one side or another. This optimum should increase the number of people using the network and, therefore, the number of intermediations conducted via the platform. The platform's main goal is to expand on the axis of quantity.

The starting point for this pricing is the different price elasticities of demand on each side. As Figure 3.5 shows, the demand curve of the households is flatter, and the demand curve of the handyworkers is steeper. In the context of this network, the households are price-elastic. Lowering their price makes sense. With a lower price, they increase the quantity they demand. This would mean that prices for handypeople should go up, as their demand is more inelastic. Following this logic, raising their prices leads them to reduce the quantity they demand, reducing the network's reach.

But here is where the indirect networks effect kicks in. Lowering prices for households leads them to expand their demand for intermediation via the platform. Raising prices for handypeople leads them to reduce their demand for intermediation. However, the platform becomes more valuable to handyworkers as household demand increases. As it increases its value, handypeople are willing to pay more for intermediation while expanding the quantity they demand.

As the handyworkers pay more, the platform can lower the price for households even more, expanding the demanded quantity again. This feedbacks into the other market side, increasing the platform's value for handypeople, making them willing to pay even more for intermediation and expand their quantity again. Once the network effect creates a feedback loop, as described here, the platform expands until reaching its saturation point, as explained in Chapter 2.

Let us see again how the effect goes from one side to the other.

Figure 3.6 shows how pricing with network effects works. It starts with the same graph as in Figure 3.5. On the left, we have the market for households and on the right for handyworkers. The price is per unit, that is, per transaction conducted via the platform. The quantity indicates the number of transactions conducted via the platform. On both sides, the supply function reflects the network's sponsor.

In the left graph, the demand curve remains unchanged and unmoved. However, the network's sponsor shifts its supply curve to the right, lowering the transaction price from Pa to Pan. The intermittent line parallel to the one called *platform supply new* gives the former supply curve. Because of the price elasticity of the supply, a price reduction leads to an overproportionate increase in quantity, as shown by the shift from Qa to Qan. Pan and Qan are the new equilibrium in this market, and Pan is the low price charged to households matching up with handyworkers on this platform.

The dotted curve indicates the network effect. The increase in demand for intermediation on the side of households makes the network more valuable to handyworkers. In the right graph, the supply remains unchanged while the demand curve shifts to the right. The former demand line is still indicated by the intermittent line parallel to the one called *demand handyworkers new*. As there is more demand from households, handyworkers seek to address this demand by expanding theirs and being matched by the network. Their expansion of demand for intermediation causes the price to rise for them from formerly Pb to Pbn. This is not a problem because, as a relatively inelastic side, handyworkers absorb the price increase.

Reducing the price of the price-elastic demand line is the best way to maximize the use of indirect network effects.

Note that the increase in quantity on the one side is achieved without any change in the platform's value proposition. It is merely a reaction to the price reduction based on the previous benefit calculation. Yet this reaction, that is, the expansion, changes the benefit perception of the other side, leading to a change in the demand function on this second side. That is how the indirect network effect works.

The platform can implement indirect network effects on the one side by utilizing price elasticity on the other. The price was lowered on one side, which increased the quantity. This makes the platform more beneficial for the other side, increasing both the price and the quantity on this second side. This effect more than compensates for the price reduction on the first side. Using elasticity and network effects in pricing, platforms create value.

The total returns TR in this case are:

$$TR = (Pan \bullet Qan) = (Pbn \bullet Qbn)$$

In any case, when using elasticity and network effects:

$$(Pan \bullet Qan) + (Pbn \bullet Qbn) > (Pa \bullet Qa) + (Pb \bullet Qb)$$

And finally, the value added is:

To implement this pricing, a network's sponsor must be able to determine the price elasticities of the demand or the sides being intermediated. Most platforms experiment quite a bit before they find a solution for pricing. Airbnb has published the main components of its formula. It is not a pricing formula per se, but it shows how elasticity and network effects are handled and summarizes many features that have been reviewed so far. It reads:

$$B = A \bullet S^\gamma \bullet D^\alpha$$

- B is the number of bookings. It is the dependent variable to be explained here. As we saw before, increasing quantity is at the heart of the platform business model.
- A is a parameter quantifying Airbnb's connection effectiveness in a specific market. It measures how well Airbnb establishes

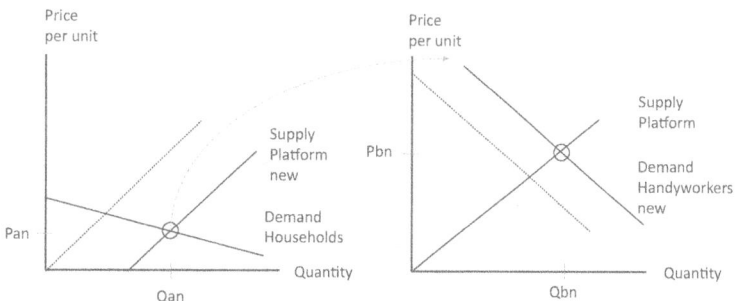

Figure 3.6 Pricing with indirect network effects (own illustration)

connections between the market sides. This is the variable we discussed in Chapter 2, the effectiveness of the intermediation.

- S is the supply of residential properties. From the perspective of Airbnb, S represents a demand for connections from those people offering accommodation.
- D is the demand for residential properties. From the perspective of Airbnb, it is the demand from customers looking for accommodation and, therefore, seeking intermediation via the platform.
- S and D both demand intermediations.
- The gamma γ is the price elasticity of demand for intermediation on the part of those supplying accommodation and demanding intermediation for that.
- The alpha α is the price elasticity of those in demand for accommodation and demanding intermediation.
- Airbnb will not publish the specific values for the individual components of the formula.

3.7 An Analytical Model

Let us finish this pricing discussion by integrating the different aspects we saw into an analytical model. We will continue with the example introduced before, HNDWK, but we changed some of its characteristics. This section will take you step by step into the modeling. The steps are:

1. declaring assumptions;
2. defining benefit functions;
3. determining the value-added VA by the platform;
4. setting the prices using the naïve approach;
5. pricing with elasticity and network effects;
6. subsidizing;
7. concluding.

Step 1: Declaring Assumptions

- The platform consists of its sponsor, the side of households, and the side of handyworkers.
- There are three households and three handyworkers.
- Each household is connected to each handyperson once.
- Both sides of the market benefit from the intermediation.
- The benefit to the households per intermediation is 2; 2 is a model counting unit for benefits.
- There are three handyworkers named 1, 2, and 3. The benefit of Handyworkers 1, 2, and 3 amounts to 1, 2, and 3, respectively, model counting units for the benefits.
- The platform's sponsor charges each side a fee for intermediating the transaction in the amount of A for households and B for handyworkers. Consequently, A and B are the prices for transacting via the platform.
- We will not look at other costs, benefits, or prices.

Step 2: Defining Benefit Functions

For households, the benefit function (and therefore, the demand function for the network's intermediation) is:

$$UH = (3 - A) \bullet s$$

- Remember, 3 is the units of benefit for the intermediation, an A is the price households pay per intermediation.
- Lowercase s is the number of handyworkers on the other side of the platform capturing the indirect network effect.
- Let us assume all households have the same benefit function.

The benefit function of the handyworkers (and, therefore, the demand function for the network's intermediation) depends on their skills. It is different for each person:

Handyworker 1: $U1 = (1 - B) \bullet n$
Handyworker 2: $U2 = (2 - B) \bullet n$

Handyworker 3: $U3 = (3 - B) \bullet n$

- Remember, the values 1, 2, and 3 are the benefit units generated by intermediation, and B is the price handyworkers pay for intermediation.
- Lowercase n is the number of households on the other side of the platform capturing the indirect network effect.

Step 3: Determining the Value-Added Va by the Platform

Putting all the intermediations of the platform together, we arrive at

$$VA = (A + B) \bullet s \bullet n$$

Step 4: Naive Pricing

In the case of the household with their homogeneous demand function, the network's sponsor or supplier can make any price <3. Three units are the household's benefit. Any price that does not absorb all the benefits still lets households enjoy some of their benefits. This is because as long as the net benefits of the households are greater than 0, they will continue to use the network.

In the case of the handyworkers, the platform increases its revenue by setting the price that maximizes it, which is 2, so $B = 2$ units of benefits. In this case, Handyperson 1 exits the platform because their benefit was 1 unit. With a price of 2 on this side, only six intermediations occur, with two handyworkers each for the three households.

In this case, the value added by the platform is:

$$VA = (A + B) \bullet s \bullet n = (3 + 2) \bullet 2 \bullet 3 = 30$$

Step 5: Pricing With Elasticity and Network Effects

The difference between demand functions should make the platform reflect and determine which side is less elastic. The handyworkers' side —in this part of the example—starting with the value of 1 unit is a strong indication of its elasticity. In contrast, the households' homogeneity of benefit at three units indicates a less price-elastic demand. Therefore, it makes sense to lower the price for handyworkers.

The platform sets $A = 2$ for households and $B = 1$ for handyworkers. On the side of handyworkers, the platform makes less revenue. Under naive pricing, it charged 2 units for six transactions, which is 12 units. Now, it is 1 unit for nine intermediations or 9 units. The answer to why the platform would lower its income is the expansion of quantity. Before, only two handyworkers were on the platform, and only six intermediations were conducted. Now, we are at nine intermediations with three handyworkers and three households.

How does this impact households? The platform's value increases on the household side because 9 intermediation times 3 units is more than 6 intermediation times 3 units. Even if the net benefit is calculated, that is, the price of 2 units is taken from the benefit of 3 units, nine is still better than six.

Taking advantage of network effects and price elasticity, the value added by the platform is:

$$VA = (2+3) \cdot 3 \cdot 3 = 45$$

This result is better than the one under naive pricing. Reducing the price on the relatively elastic side of the platform triggers indirect network effects, which increase activity on the platform, benefiting both sides and the whole network.

Step 6: Subsidizing

A notable feature of network economics is that it can go further than price differentiation. *Price differentiation* means that different prices exist for the same good or service. These prices are made to fit a person's willingness to pay or elasticity. Subsidization takes this one step further. One market side pays for the other. This means that one market side has a zero or negative price, balanced out by the other.

- To showcase this, we will have to change our model a bit:

- The platform connects six households with six handyworkers.
- The benefit function of the households is $UH = (6 - A) \cdot s$
- The benefit function of the handyworkers is: i represents the individual benefit accruing to each handyworker, $i = 1, 2, \ldots, 6$.
- These benefit functions mean Handyworkers 1 and 2 do not participate in the network. Their benefit function has a –3. This means their benefit would be negative even with the price $B = 0$.
- The households, as the relatively inelastic side, pay the price $A = 5$.

Let us put this together:

Let the price on the handyworkers' side be $B = 2$. Only two of them would use the network. Handyworker 5, $U\% = (5 - 3 - 2) * n$ and Handyworker 6, $U6 = (6 - 3 - 2) * n$. The result of the benefit function is negative for the other four, meaning that they do not use the platform. Twelve intermediations occur with the prices $A = 6$ and $B = 2$; this results from six households and two handyworkers. The value added of the platform is:

$$VA = (5 + 2) \cdot 2 \cdot 6 = 84$$

The side of the handyworkers is the relatively elastic one. The platform could make it free for handyworkers to use its intermediation. If $B = 0$, then four handyworkers take part in the platform. This increases the number of intermediations to 24, or 4 times 6. Value creation increases to:

$$VA = (5 + 0) \cdot 3 \cdot 6 = 90$$

Lowering the price on one side also results in indirect network effects and, therefore, higher added value. Even if one side pays no prices and thereby reduces that side's revenue to zero, the indirect network effects can compensate for this. The revenues from the other side overcompensate for the one-sided effect and result in greater value creation.

Can we subsidize one side with a negative price, that is, paying for that side to participate? Let us see. Lowering the price for handyworkers to $B = -1$ increases the number of intermediations from 24 to 30, or 5 times 6. The overall value added of the platform is:

$$VA = (5 - 1) \cdot 5 \cdot 6 = 120$$

Reducing B to $B = -2$ increases the number of intermediations to 36, which is 6 times 6. In this case, the value added of the platform is

$$VA = (5 - 2) \cdot 6 \cdot 6 = 108$$

Therefore, the value added by this platform is greatest at $B = -1$. Subsidizing even more and lowering the price to include all possible handyworkers extends the platform's reach. However, it does not necessarily increase the value added to the platform. There is only so much one side can pay to the other. There is an optimum amount of subsidy, which in this example is $B = -1$.

A last word about the side of households: It is correct that this side pays for the other side. However, this does not occur at their expense. Households experience a net benefit in any configuration of this network and its prices. Even when paying for the other side, the households benefit from the expanding network, and their price is below their willingness to pay.

Step 7: Concluding

Lowering prices to zero, making negative prices, or generally subsidizing one side through the other can increase value creation in the network by triggering indirect network effects. This does not mean, however, that the maximum possible network expansion by means of zero and negative prices always leads to greater value creation. The network is at its optimum size when the value creation of the entire network is at its maximum.

3.8 Price Differentiation and Dynamic Prices

We are done with analytical modeling for now. However, practical concerns regarding pricing still need to be addressed. In platform business models, pricing is much more differentiated and dynamic, especially in the digital world. To study these terms, it is helpful to distinguish three degrees of their granularity, starting with the most detailed:

First-Degree Price Differentiation

First-degree price differentiation, also known as first-degree price discrimination or perfect price discrimination, occurs when a seller charges each consumer the maximum price they are willing to pay for a product or service. The seller needs detailed information about each consumer's willingness to pay, which is challenging to achieve in practice but can be approximated through various strategies.

In markets where haggling is common, such as car dealerships or bazaars, sellers often negotiate with buyers to determine the highest price each buyer is willing to pay. This results in varying final prices based on negotiation skills and perceived value. Online retailers and platforms can use data analytics and consumer behavior tracking to offer personalized prices, analyzing a user's browsing history, purchase patterns, and demographic information to tailor product prices.

Some businesses, such as airlines and ride-sharing services, use dynamic pricing algorithms to adjust prices in real time based on demand, availability, and individual consumer data, allowing them to charge different prices to different consumers based on their willingness to pay at a given moment. In an auction setting, the winning bidder pays the highest price they are willing to pay for an item, closely approximating first-degree price discrimination as each bidder reveals their maximum willingness to pay through their bids.

Implementing first-degree price discrimination requires detailed knowledge of each consumer's willingness to pay, which is often difficult to obtain accurately. Additionally, consumers may perceive individualized pricing as unfair or discriminatory, potentially leading to dissatisfaction or backlash against the seller. In some jurisdictions, price discrimination practices are regulated or restricted to prevent unfair treatment of consumers.

Dynamic Pricing

Dynamic pricing is a technique for differentiation of the first degree. It is very popular with digital business models because digital algorithms make it easy to adjust prices in real time, which is the core of dynamic pricing. Currently, there are four significant ways in which dynamic pricing is made:

- *Power shopping*: In this model, the seller sets price levels based on the quantity demanded. Consumers respond by purchasing a certain quantity, and the predetermined price is based on the total quantity demanded. This allows consumers to react collectively and decide on a price as a group. By joining together, consumers can achieve market power despite dealing with large quantities.
- *Reverse auction*: In a reverse auction, the buyer places an order and, if applicable, an indicative price. Sellers respond to this order, and if the information flow allows, their bids are made public so they can adjust their offers accordingly. Ultimately, only one bid satisfies the demand.
- *Reverse pricing*: This method allows buyers to pay the prices they consider fair. Sellers can provide cost indications, set price thresholds, or disclose prices paid by other buyers, ensuring that all consumers are accommodated.
- *Auction*: In a traditional auction, the product or service is sold to the highest bidder.

Second-Degree Price Differentiation

This type of differentiation occurs when a seller charges different prices based on the quantity or quality of the product or service rather than identifying distinct groups of consumers. In this form of price differentiation, the price varies according to the amount consumed or the version of the product chosen, allowing consumers to self-select into different pricing tiers based on their preferences and needs. It can take many forms, for example:

- Differentiation according to the quantity purchased (larger quantity at a lower price per unit), newness (so-called skimming: If a product or service is new on the market, its price is higher, but the longer it remains on the market, the lower its price), or versioning is typical.

- Versioning plays an essential role in networks. Since the OPEX of most networks is low to zero, different versions of the same network will hardly result in cost changes. They can, however, result in considerable differences in revenues. The idea is to give customers as much choice as possible on all sides to ensure they find the best prices that reflect their willingness to pay. Some examples of this are:

  Freemium: Depending on the version and service level, users pay nothing (free) or a fee (premium).

  Service level: Users can determine which service level they want and pay a price based on that level.

  Lock-in: Users pay a low or no price during the initial phase of their membership to the network. Once they have made themselves at home in the network, the network sets them a price for use. This is higher than zero but lower than the switching costs. As a result, the user remains locked in, that is, they pay the price but have no incentive to leave the network. Another version of the same effect involves the user paying to join the network. Once the access costs have been paid, the user is less willing to leave the network.

- *Bundling*: Users can join several parts of the network by paying a flat rate or an all-in price.

Bundling and Unbundling Software

A software company produces a word processing program, T, and a spreadsheet program, K. The production costs of the individual programs are zero. There are four consumers with different willingness to pay:

Customer A is prepared to pay 10 dollars for T and 90 dollars for K. Customer B is willing to pay 40 dollars for T and 80 dollars for K. Customer C is prepared to pay 80 dollars for T and 40 dollars for K. Customer D is prepared to pay 90 dollars for T and 10 dollars for K.

How can we use bundling in this context?

- Unbundling, selling T and K separately. If the price for each program is set at 80 dollars each, then A and B buy program T, and C and D buy program K. The total revenue is 320 dollars.
- Pure bundling means offering both products together and, in doing so, relying on the lowest sum of preferences, that is, willingness to pay for T and K. The sum of A's and D's preferences is 100 dollars and of B and C is 120 dollars. If the bundling price is 100 dollars, all customers buy both programs. The total revenue is 400 dollars.
- Mixed bundling means offering both the programs individually and in a bundle. The individual price reflects the customer's highest remaining willingness to pay. The price for bundling corresponds to the sum of the willingness to pay of the others. So, if the price of the individual programs is 90 dollars each and the bundling price is 120, then A buys T, D buys K, and B and C buy both in a bundle. The total revenue is 420 dollars.

Third-Degree Price Differentiation

Third-degree price differentiation is the least granular and occurs when a seller charges different prices to different groups of consumers for the same product or service. These groups are segmented based on specific characteristics such as age, location, time of purchase, or consumer behavior. The seller identifies these distinct groups and sets prices accordingly to maximize revenue and profits. Examples include student discounts, geographic, time-based, or member pricing.

3.9 Practical Pricing Strategies

Let us finish this chapter by going through the most common pricing strategies implemented by online platforms; they are:

- free;
- freemium (including subscription and credit based);
- pay-per-use (including as a service);
- long tail;
- marketplace.

Free

One side pays nothing; the willingness of advertisers to pay is maximized. Many major Internet companies launched their business model exclusively with free services or still offer their services (essentially) free of charge today, such as Facebook, Google, YouTube, Craigslist, and many online newspapers.

The benefit of this model is the potential to gain people and market share quickly. Internet users are often more sensitive to prices than others due to the high price transparency on the web and the many free services. If they get something for free, they usually take it without thinking twice.

Even if base content is free, revenue can be generated through premium additional services purchased and paid for by a proportion of customers (see Freemium below). On the other hand, there are models financed purely by advertising.

The internet holds several advantages over traditional advertising media in terms of advertising since messages can be conveyed in a much more targeted manner. Digital platforms and ecosystems collect data on the people using them. These data may interest advertisers so they can achieve the most targeted and personalized approach possible. This means less scatter loss for advertisers and, therefore, higher efficiency.

Digital platforms and ecosystems can differentiate their prices in two ways to maximize their revenues by targeting advertisers' willingness to pay:

- The first possibility is price differentiation by the target person. This is because the more targeted the approach, the higher the price of advertising that can be achieved. If we look at Facebook, for example, providers looking to create an advertisement can narrow down their target group by country, demographics, education, and interests. The more precisely the target group is defined, the higher the achievable cost per thousand contacts (CPM) or cost per click (CPC).
- The second possibility of advertising price differentiation, like Google AdWords, functions based on the advertised content or product. A more attractive keyword is given a higher price than one less in demand. The auction mechanism for price determination has become prevalent on such platforms, irrespective of price differentiation. Depending on the specified target group or keywords, a CPM or CPC price range is suggested to the advertiser, at which the advertiser can submit a bid. With the CPC model, the advertiser only pays when clicking the banner ad. An algorithm calculates which ads are shown to the customer based on the price offered and the likelihood of a click. This maximizes the advertising revenue.

Freemium

Introduce people to the network free of charge and then convert them into paying members within a certain period. This is known as conversion. The problem with free is that revenue is generated exclusively from advertising, which leads to a high dependency on the advertising (price) market. The freemium model seeks to find a solution.

Freemium means that the people using the network can do so free of charge, but they can choose to purchase additional paid services.

Examples of this include XING, LinkedIn, Dropbox, and Doodle. All the networks referred to above offer a free basic membership plus one or more types of paid premium memberships. These comprise the basic membership services and attractive additional services offered to network users. The person wishing to do so concludes a contract with the provider, which generally runs for 3 to 12 months, paying a fixed monthly basic amount.

However, based on monthly subscriptions, the freemium model also has drawbacks. For one thing, many people using the network tend to shy away from making a long-term commitment to a network and the associated conclusion of a contract. This pushes down the conversion rate and the proportion of people using the paid service version. Second, there are often so-called power users or fans willing to pay significantly more than the monthly subscription—but due to the existing pricing model, this willingness to pay is not exploited.

Due to these restrictions, another freemium pricing model is becoming more attractive: the *à la carte* model involving payment in advance. *À la carte* freemium models work with prepaid one-off transactions and have already become standard in online gaming. Like with the subscription model, players can play the game for free for as long as they like. They also have the chance to buy additional credits. They can then exchange these credits for additional services, such as equipment to strengthen their character in online gaming, magic potions to advance faster, or so-called vanity items to visually stand out from the crowd of players.

The *à la carte* freemium pricing model is particularly effective in networks where the people using the network are emotionally invested and have a high level of involvement. Such is the case, for example, regarding online gaming, dating services, or betting sites. This model allows users to purchase as many credits and services as they wish. This means the willingness to pay off real fans and intensive users is fully exploited. Experience shows that the average revenue per paying user is often over 50 dollars per user per month in the gaming sector.

There are also hybrid models comprising subscriptions and credits. The social network Badoo offers its users a superpower subscription, whereby users are provided with some premium services on an ongoing basis (such as access to more profiles). In contrast, other functions are only provided when credits are purchased and used (such as temporarily better placement in searches). The payment trigger is decisive for the success of freemium—whether it is subscription or credit based. These are features of the network or events for which people using the network are willing to pay.

Pay-Per-Use

People using the network pay for the connection established via the network or for each transaction mediated via the network. This pricing model is more akin to the classic equilibrium market model. The connection or intermediation is the product or service converted into money. Telephone networks have long been organized around this principle. You paid for the individual connection or for how long the individual connection lasted. Services providing a ride, such as Juno, charge a commission for a completed journey.

The benefits of this model lie in its directness and transparency. Such models are simple and understandable, especially in networks where one-off transactions for homogeneous goods are brokered. The disadvantage is that the willingness to pay is only exploited once. Continuous interaction in the network in this model depends heavily on the people using it.

A form of pay-per-use that is currently frequently used is Anything as a Service. XaaS denotes that fixed or durable goods are also under the pay-per-use pricing mechanism. Taking the example of a pipeline business model, buying a copying device is unnecessary. It can remain the property of the manufacturer. The manufacturer places the machine on the customer's premises and charges a price per copy generated. Taking the example of a non-digital network, public entities do not need to buy street lamps. These remain the property of the lamp manufacturer, who also takes over the maintenance of the lamps. The municipality remunerates the lamp manufacturer for the energy used by the lamps to light the streets.

Long Tail

You are exploiting willingness to pay for niche products. The long tail theory suggests that niche products can be profitable precisely in the internet age. In the case of physical goods, niche products are problematic because they tie down capital, take up storage space, and entail certain risks. These are all cost factors. In contrast, these three cost drivers do not apply to digital and network goods.

The theory of the long tail, therefore, emphasizes niche products instead of mass products and is based on the premise that niche products can be particularly important for the economic success of a company because of the opportunities that the internet brings with it. The reason behind this is that anyone can offer any conceivable product on the internet at a low cost—and these highly specialized products usually attract other people who are willing to buy them.

In other words, the internet offers the ideal platform for niche products to succeed in the long tail. Selling many niche products probably leads to higher sales than a few bestsellers in an international context. Many digital media providers like iTunes or Netflix have adopted this business model. Apple offers over 12 million songs for download or as a service in its iTunes Store (based on its figures), including many niche products with manageable sales.

Products that are available practically everywhere often face tough price and margin pressure. This is why many retailers try to attract (new) customers by setting rock-bottom prices for popular electrical goods or other focus products. This does not apply to niche products: Competitive prices are not worth it here since most customers do not notice them or find them of no interest. On the contrary, the reduced number of suppliers combined with the increased search costs for the customer means that the willingness to pay for niche products is frequently higher than for comparable products with a higher footfall.

The long tail approach relies on a statistical distribution, as shown in Figure 3.7. The allocation has a head comprising about 20 percent of the quantity but 80 percent of the value. Its long tail comprises 80 percent of the quantity but only 20 percent of the value of the products and services in a market. Based on the long tail theory, the value share of

Value

Head   Long tail
20%   80%

Quantity

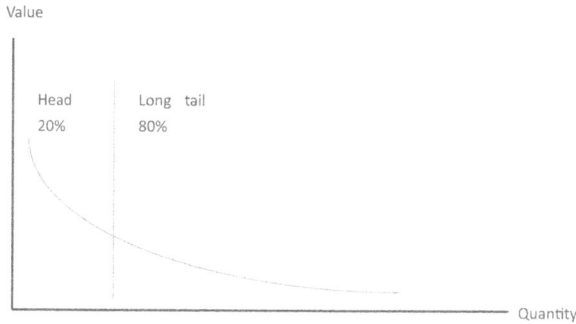

Figure 3.7 Long tail (own illustration)

this 80 percent can be increased if pricing strategies are oriented toward this long tail.

However, no empirical evidence suggests that this model is more successful than average. Nevertheless, there is sufficient evidence for the long tail fallacy. The growing availability of niche products is shifting demand toward the long tail. The long tail is, therefore, becoming longer and thinner. This means, however, that the head of the distribution is also getting thinner and, crucially, higher. In other words, the increasing availability of various niche products drives demand toward polarization. Therefore, focusing on niche products results in a concentration on the non-niche.

The Marketplace Model

Differentiate prices based on the benefits provided. The niche products that can be acquired need not necessarily be posted by the provider—as with the iTunes Store. Business models such as YouTube or Wikipedia are based on content generation by those using the network. eBay and Amazon have also been adopting this concept for over a decade. However, it has only been in recent years that it has gathered further momentum: the platform or marketplace concept, which is used for both digital and tangible goods.

Any user can offer their (niche) products on these digital marketplaces. Platforms such as eBay, Quelle, Amazon, Play, or Lulu act as sales channels and collect a fee for every transaction, which is (approximately) between 5 and 30 percent, depending on the type and value of the product. Unlike eBay, whose only function is as a platform, Amazon uses its marketplace for niche products. When a product becomes *too successful*, the online retailer adds it to its range. In doing so, Amazon combines the benefits of its own and partner sales. Around 1.3 million professional retailers sell their goods on the Amazon marketplace today. Marketplace strategies facilitate a low-risk business model for the marketplace operator since the costs for procurement, warehousing, and shipping of the goods are outsourced to the retailer.

Let us take Apple as an example: The App Store, launched in 2008, allows owners of Apple hardware to browse over 500,000 different apps for the iPhone, iPod touch, or iPad. As of October 2011, over 18 billion (!) users had downloaded apps. Most apps are not developed by Apple but by independent programmers. Apple receives a 30 percent revenue share for every app sold. Force.com has been equally successful in the B2B sector, offering over 1,200 apps and over one million downloads.

Yet, marketplaces are not a surefire success. A critical mass must also be achieved on all sites connected by the network. Let us take Skype as an example: The online video service reports over 650 million registered users, around 50 million of whom go online daily. Despite this, the critical mass has not been attained in various additional services—even at zero prices.

The right pricing strategy can potentially help selectively develop the number of providers. As with all business models that rely on critical mass, it is advisable to enter the market at low fees and gradually increase them. That is why smaller/younger marketplaces like Hitmeister or Hood have lower fee levels than eBay or Amazon.

On top of a price level increase over time, taking a more differentiated stance on the seller's business model is also advisable. For example, electronics sellers on Amazon and eBay pay lower sales fees than those selling watches or jewelry. The pricing model reflects the margin and the turnover rate of the products. A sales commission to the platform of 20 percent is appropriate for jewelry sales with a high margin but lower turnover; in the case of electronic goods with a lower margin and high turnover rate, 5 percent is appropriate.

Prices can also be broken down by region using the same principle, depending on the value of the service. The leading American classifieds portal Craigslist offers most of its services free of charge—with some exceptions: Posting a job ad in the San Francisco area costs $75, and $25 in New York and eight other cities. Property ads are free across the country—except in New York, where realtors and homeowners are charged 10 dollars for their ads.

The German real estate exchange ImmobilienScout24 uses a similar approach to pricing and breaks down its prices into four regions. Good properties in Munich (as in New York) are in short supply, for example, and demand is high. The chance of renting out the apartment quickly (and thereby collecting two months' rent as commission) is extremely good for the realtor. Someone who wants to advertise a house or apartment here will pay a higher price than someone who advertises a comparable property in Cottbus (with less chance of a comparable commission).

3.10 Critical Assessment

Setting prices is a dynamic process. Models can only provide a snapshot, if at all. They are unable to deal with the dynamics. This is better explored in practice, that is, by applying pricing strategies and experimenting with pricing mechanisms.

However, models are still valuable. They operationalize economic theory and systematize economic parameters regarding their relationship. As such, models can examine cause-and-effect relationships. To do so, however, they require abstract assumptions. Models serve as instruments for understanding exchange relationships. By contrast, models are unable to explain what happens. Not even analytical models can comprehend reality as a whole in their equations, nor can they make a forecast.

Models, nonetheless, can have a practical benefit. They can help network providers gain an understanding of how prices are set. This understanding provides information and facilitates their decisions. The models can help these providers realize various factors influencing pricing. Price setting involves a discovery process, with network providers repeatedly adjusting their pricing mechanisms to suit those of the network users. It frequently takes networks years to find a stable pricing mechanism. In many cases, pricing is adjusted as the network develops and expands.

Setting prices must be seen in the context of network governance. Pricing for connection or intermediation constitutes only one aspect of a network's broader institutions. These include rules on the system's openness, building trust between participants, resolving conflicts, and coping with changing situations. The rules on pricing can be added to this list as a fifth element. This broader concept of network governance is outlined in Chapter 4.

In any event, the following applies: While correct pricing is a prerequisite for implementing (indirect) network effects, it alone is not enough. Sophisticated governance is crucial for networks. It ensures that network effects can be implemented over the long term, making business models more robust and reliable. This means that governance is a sufficient prerequisite for networks—without it, nothing works.

Summary

- The network connects different people or groups of people.
- The economic value creation of a network is the sum of the prices these people or groups pay for these connections and the resulting transactions.
- Pricing is a discovery process: Suppliers discover consumers' value assessments, and consumers discover suppliers' cost structures. This takes place through an infinite number of interactions, reactions, and counter-reactions.
- The market is a feedback mechanism. Price is one of the ways the market process provides feedback to people.
- Economics conceives prices as the result of a market process. Supply and demand agree on a price and a quantity. This agreement is called equilibrium and maximizes the welfare of people in a market.

- In a network business model, the network's sponsor is the supplier of intermediation. The people using the network are the demand for intermediation.
- Naive pricing uses the market equilibrium approach to pricing in network business models. This approach fails to include network effects in the pricing strategy.
- Price elasticity of demand denotes the sensitivity of demand to price changes. A price-elastic demand changes the quantity demanded overproportionate to changes in price, while a price-inelastic demand changes the quantity underproportionate to the change in price.
- The more possibility for substitution, the more price-elastic demand is.
- A more nuanced view of networks uses differences in elasticity to trigger indirect network effects. Using different elasticities means following a network pricing strategy.
- If prices are lowered for the more price-elastic group, then the number of people in this group increases. This also makes the network more attractive and prompts people from other groups to join, who then pay higher prices, in turn. As a result, the value creation of the entire network increases.
- Pricing for the more price-elastic group can result in zero or negative price differentiation.
- Various models for pricing in networks have become established in practice. The most common include free, freemium, pay-per-use (including as a service), long tail, and marketplace.
- Pricing is a necessary element for the governance of networks, although it is not sufficient on its own.
- The next chapter addresses the governance of network business models.

Review Questions

First Series: Which Statements Are Correct? Which Are Not?

1. The price is an objective measure of the value of a commodity.

2. Prices are dynamic variables; they fluctuate depending on the situation.
3. In equilibrium markets, equilibrium prices maximize the benefit of those participating.
4. Naive pricing in networks determines prices in the same way as equilibrium models.
5. The direct network effects are included in pricing with network effects.
6. In pricing with network effects, the price is lowered on the price-inelastic side.
7. Zero and negative prices are not possible in networks.
8. Zero and negative prices in networks always increase the entire benefit of the network.
9. The maximum network expansion does not always result in the maximum benefit of the network.
10. In the case of price differentiation, the prices of the commodities are adjusted in line with the suppliers' willingness to pay.

Second Series: Solve the Following Challenges

1. If the price of a commodity increases by 9 percent, the quantity demanded decreases by 7 percent. Is it a commodity that is price-elastic or price-inelastic? Is this price increase worthwhile for the supplier who wants to increase their profit? Why?
2. A company sells 12,000 sweets for 12 cents each. It lowers the price of the sweets to 10 cents each. Assuming the price elasticity of demand is 1.35, what sales volume can the company expect? What effect will this price change have on profits?
3. A platform connects two sides. One side is made up of people who help with removals, and the other side is made up of people who move. The first side is more price-elastic. Outline the pricing of this platform by implementing network effects and illustrate the economic effect of this implementation.
4. Explain the pricing strategy free online newspapers use concerning price setting with network effects.

5. A platform connects people who help with homework and people who need help. The benefit functions are as follows:
   a. Homework help 1 $U = (3-B) * n$
   b. Homework help 2 $U = (4-B) * n$
   c. Homework help 3 $U = (5-B) * n$
   d. Homework assignments 1, 2, and 3 $U = (3A) * s$
   e. U denotes benefit, B is the fee that the side providing homework help must pay for successful intermediation, and A is the fee for those doing homework. The number of people on this site is n; the number of homework helpers is s.
   f. Set the price that maximizes the value creation of the platform.

6. An online platform comprises two areas. People who are studying and people who are not studying participate in the platform. Using the information below, set prices according to the following principles: unit price, versioning, third-degree differentiation, versioning, and third-degree differentiation—however, each person only buys one version:
   a. Person 1 is not studying and pays 20 dollars for the standard version and 25 for the premium.
   b. Person 2 is not studying and pays 18 dollars for the standard version and 24 for the premium.
   c. Person 3 is not studying and pays 15 dollars for the standard version and 23 for the premium.
   d. Person 4 is not studying and pays 14 dollars for the standard version and 18 for the premium.
   e. Person 5 is not studying and pays 9 dollars for the standard version and 10 for the premium.
   f. Person 6 is not studying and pays 5 dollars for the standard version and five for the premium.
   g. Person 7 is studying and pays 15 dollars for the standard version and 17 for the premium.
   h. Person 8 is studying and pays 14 dollars for the standard version and 15 for the premium.

   i.   Person 9 is studying and pays 10 dollars for the standard
        version and 12 for the premium.

   j.   Person 10 is studying and pays 8 dollars for the standard
        version and 9 for the premium.

   k.   Person 11 is studying and pays four dollars for the standard
        version and five for the premium.

   l.   Person 12 is studying and pays three dollars for the standard
        version and four for the premium.

7. Explain the pricing of PlayStation.

8. Explain the pricing of OkCupid.

9. Which consequences do the practical pricing models, free and
   freemium, have on the maximum network size? Formulate
   corresponding hypotheses.

10. How would lock-in and freemium be applied in practice? Look
    for an example.

Third series: Respond to the Following Questions and Solve the Mini-Case Studies

1. Develop an analytical, numerical example by demonstrating how
   zero and negative prices implement indirect network effects to
   maximize the network optimum.

2. Develop a numerical example demonstrating how bundling and
   unbundling function and their effect on value creation.

3. Develop the pricing structure of a non-digital network with two
   sides.

4. Develop the pricing structure of a digital network with three
   sides.

5. Find an example of a long tail and a marketplace pricing model
   and explain how they vary.

6. Find an example of a free and a freemium pricing model and
   explain how they vary.

7. Use an example you researched to explain the *long tail fallacy*.

8. Why are the pricing options for non-digital networks limited?

9. What are the similarities and differences between pricing in markets and networks?

10. Use your own words to explain the difference between the explanatory and the understanding function of models in economic theory.

Commented Bibliography

- De Reuver, M., C. Sørensen, and R.C. Basole. 2018. "The Digital Platform: A Research Agenda." *Journal of Information Technology* 33(2): 124–135.
  - A research article in which current and future fields of research on online networks are outlined.
- Knieps, G. 2016. *Network Economics*. Springer Verlag.
  - A comprehensive introduction to pricing in English.
- Mansell, R. and W.E. Steinmueller. 2020. *Advanced Introduction to Platform Economics*. Edward Elgar Publishing.
  - This book for advanced readers builds on this chapter's foundations and incorporates the overarching aspects of network economics, such as artificial intelligence and globalization.
- Øverby, H. and J. Audestad. 2021. *Introduction to Digital Economics: Foundations, Business Models and Case Studies*. Springer Verlag.
  - Very detailed introduction to the economic laws of networks and a good connection between economic theory and business administration, including their applications.
- Veile, J.W., M.C. Schmidt, and K.I. Voigt. 2022. "Toward a New Era of Cooperation: How Industrial Digital Platforms Transform Business Models in Industry 4.0." *Journal of Business Research* 143: 387–405.
  - A comprehensive review of strategy, business model, and pricing regarding digital platforms in the industry sector.

CHAPTER 4

Governance

This chapter focuses on the governance of networks. Governance refers to the processes and rules that standardize the behavior of those involved in the network. Governance is essential for networks; it is a critical factor in the service architecture since the network's trust, connections, stability, robustness, and resilience depend on it. Governance is fundamental for network effects to take effect. This chapter draws on many practical and theoretical observations that have been made in implementing network economics in business management over recent years. This chapter concludes with a critical assessment, an outlook on future developments, and research desiderata. After reading this chapter, you will be able to:

- Section 4.1: define governance in the context of networks.
- Section 4.2: gain an overview of the elements of governance.
- Section 4.3: explain the interplay of the elements of governance in network business models.
- Section 4.4: discuss the importance of access and control for networks.
- Section 4.5: use systems aimed at increasing trust and mitigating risks.
- Section 4.6: apply signaling and sanctioning.
- Section 4.7: recognize the problems in the transfer of reputation.
- Section 4.8: understand what makes networks strong.
- Section 4.9: create different governance strategies for network business models.

> • Section 4.10: assess the contents of this chapter critically.

4.1 Governance: Managing Connections

The network's business model involves establishing connections and facilitating transactions. This requires an operational structure that makes the connections possible and ensures they are permanent. It also requires tools for generating revenue from these connections or the transactions resulting from them to generate income or revenue.

Chapter 2 reviewed the selection of target groups and the establishment of connections, and Chapter 3 discussed generating revenue via pricing. Now, we need to organize the connection, intermediation, and transaction. This is compliance's job. Once we've done that, we will have reviewed all the components of the business model as introduced in Chapter 1.

The basic structure of the business model comprises target groups, the value proposition, the implementation architecture, and the revenue management. In pipeline business models, the implementation architecture ensures the integration of suppliers, production program planning, the organization of work within the company, the implementation of marketing activities, or the distribution and quality controls.

Since all these tasks and processes are led by management and follow the rules and standards developed by management, they could be called governance. However, in pipeline business models, they are usually referred to as operations. Indeed, the word governance is only used in its more legal meaning in pipelines. It entails the legal framework and control of managerial and executive activities to fulfill the corporate purpose and appropriately involve shareholders and stakeholders. Governance in this legal sense follows four principles: accountability, responsibility, transparency, and fairness.

In network business models, the story is different. Governance, that is, setting up rules and processes, is at the core of such business models because governance enables intermediation and transaction. Networks are about bringing people together. These people must be incentivized to transact, trust each other, and use the platform. Governance is crucial for this motivation. Marshall Van Alstyne, whose works we have already referenced, puts it like this:

> We define a platform as an open architecture with governance rules to facilitate interactions. The open architecture allows third parties to come in and add value. The governance rules motivate them to come in and add value, and then the interactions create value. Without the interactions, you don't get the ride, the tweet, or the auction purchase. You need all of the interactions that actually create value. You use the governance model to motivate more healthy interactions and to mitigate unhealthy interactions (Interview at Summit Health Advisors 2024)

Governance is the main element of the implementation architecture in platform business models. We will define the term as a system of rules and processes for controlling a network to create and sustain connections. Network governance aims to implement network effects to benefit all participants.

As we have seen already, a network's governance addresses four desiderata, the four C's:

1. Creation: setting up, or programming, an intermediation structure, the software, algorithm, or app. Sometimes, creation is called supply. It is about the main intermediation of the platform or about precisely discerning which target groups interact via the platform.

2. Curation: setting up and enforcing the network's rules. As we will see later, an artificially created network cannot rely on customs, beliefs, and social institutions. There needs to be a robust design of rules so that people can trust that the intermediation works. Network business models involve strangers. For the intermediation to succeed, the strangers must develop trust in the network. This trust is the result of a set of clear and enforced rules.

3. Customization: engineering the benefits for the users of the network. Each user in each target group uses the network for very personal reasons. The more the user can adapt the network to their specific needs, the higher the likelihood of continuously transacting via the network.

4. Consumption: steering users of the network to interact via the network. In different networks, there is a tendency to use the platform to gain information. Once there is information, the transaction is conducted directly, that is, without the network as an intermediator. I could use a hotel platform to inform myself but then book directly with the hotel for a better price. Consumption means that the network business models engineer the implementation architecture around incentivizing the users to complete the transactions via the platform.

However, a more pressing question is how to do it. There are six elements of a platform's governance strategy to implement the four C's:

1. Governance structure involves the basic principles of a platform's governance and the responsibilities of the people in charge.

2. Access and control are decisions about who can join the network and who controls the transactions intermediated by the platform.

3. Resources and documentation are, on the one hand, about how transparent a platform is and, on the other, how much the platform helps users to get on board.

4. Trust and risk are about establishing and passing on reputation so people feel secure transacting via the network.

5. Pricing is an element of both implementation architecture and revenue mechanism.

6. External relationships are whether a platform wants to interface with other platforms or be part of an ecosystem.

In the remainder of this chapter, we will review these elements in more detail.

Table 4.1. Elements of network governance

Element	Mechanisms	Questions
Governance structure	• Decision-making rights • Owner status	Is the network centralized or decentralized/distributed? How are authority and responsibility divided between the platform's sponsor and developers of its contents or modules? Is the platform sponsored by one agent, for example, a company, or does it have multiple sponsors?
Resources and documentation	• Transparency • Platform boundary resources	Does the documentation allow for easy understanding and user-friendliness of the platform? Are governance decisions relating to joining the network and developing modules easy to follow and understand? Are application programming interfaces (APIs) or software development kits (SDKs) used to facilitate third-party application development?
Access and control	Output control and monitoring	How are outputs, for example, transactions and add-on apps, evaluated, sanctioned, or rewarded?
	• Input control • Safety	Which mechanisms are in place to control which products or services are permitted? How can the quality of services or products be assessed?
	• Accessibility • Process control • Openness	Who has access to the platform, and are there any restrictions on participation? Who controls the process and is responsible for regulation? Is the platform open or closed?
Trust and risk	• Reinforcing trust • Reducing the perceived risk	Does the platform foster the building of trust?

(Continued)

Table 4.1. (Continued)

Element	Mechanisms	Questions
		How can the perceived risk of platform participants be minimized?
Pricing	• Price structure • Subsidy • Revenue	Who sets the price? Who decides on participation, pays, and claims the value created? Who subsidized whom?
External relationships	• External relationship management	How are interdependencies between participants and other networks managed? What is the architecture of participation? Does the platform permit technical interoperability between other systems?

Source: Schreieck et al. (2018), 55.

4.2 Elements of Governance: Overview

Table 4.1 summarizes the elements of network governance. It identifies mechanisms operationalizing these elements and asks the questions associated with them. This section provides an overview of the elements while the next explains them. Three of these elements are discussed in more detail in this book. Pricing was the focus of Chapter 3; access and control will be addressed in Section "Integration"; trust and risk are the topics of Section "Trust and Risk". Keep in mind that the perspective taken here is the platform's sponsor:

The table offers an overview, but even a cursory look at the questions shows they address fundamental issues in the platform's setup. Any sponsor is well advised to answer these questions one by one. These answers are otherwise not helpful in understanding how the platform will operate. However, one advantage of digital networks is that they allow more experimentation. Sponsors can change some of their network decisions and test how the changes work out. If they increase reach, traffic, and transactions, the changes in governance can stay; if not, they can be reconsidered.

4.3 Elements of Governance: Explanation

Let us go back to the elements and mechanisms summarized in Table 4.1. This section adds some explanations, relying on Schreieck et al. (2018), 59–64.

Governance Structure

This element concerns centralized and decentralized structures, decision-making rights, and the network's ownership status.

The Google Play Store is an excellent example of the effects of a low or high level of centralization on decision-making rights. It was initially freely accessible open-source software with decentralized governance, with each developer setting their standards and rules. This approach resulted in rapid growth in the number of developers and gamers. However, it also led to tensions caused by a lack of control over the content and problems with marketing the network. This pushed Google to centralize. As its sponsor, Google implemented a set of requirements for developers that improved the quality of the games offered on the platform. However, this centralization led many developers to exit the platform. With fewer developers, the variety of games offered via Google Play Store diminished, which made it more challenging to market the network. After centralizing its governance and losing developers, the network also lost gamers.

Generally, a decentralized governance structure leads to faster growth, greater reach, and more transactions. Often, the quality of the content, the quality of the technical modules, and problems with trust go together with decentralization. Centralized structures build up a brand, have better quality content and technology, and are often more reliable. However, they need longer to grow and cannot be as easily marketed.

A centralized structure gives the network's sponsor more control over the network itself, the transactions it facilitates, and the general outcomes of connections. However, it tends to be more expensive and resource-intensive since control requires implementing tools, processes, and people. A decentralized or distributed governance structure relies on self-organization and emerging order, which can be a source of innovation and a thrust for the platform's further development. On the other hand, decentralized organizations have higher transaction costs due to information asymmetries.

An example of a centralized governance structure is Uber. One for a distributed or decentralized structure is Reddit.

Resources and Documentation

The operational aspect of how open a platform is depends on how much transparency the network's sponsor espouses or allows and which platform boundary resources are made available.

Transparency involves the sponsor openly sharing information about the platform's operations, policies, updates, and plans, which helps build trust among users and developers, fostering greater participation and innovation. It also includes making decision-making processes clear, revealing governance structures, criteria for decision-making, and feedback mechanisms so people in the network and interested in joining it can understand the rationale behind certain decisions. Additionally, sharing performance metrics and data about the platform's usage, growth, and challenges is crucial for developers and businesses to make informed decisions about engaging with the platform.

The availability of platform boundary resources is another critical aspect. This includes providing well-documented application programming interfaces (APIs), allowing external developers to build on the platform's core functionality easily. Software development kits (SDKs), which offer necessary tools, libraries, documentation, and sample code, are also crucial for enabling developers to effectively create applications for the platform. Moreover, access to support forums, community wikis, and direct support from the platform sponsor can help developers overcome challenges and share knowledge, fostering a collaborative and innovative ecosystem. Transparent and fair licensing terms and terms of use define how third parties can interact with and build on the platform, with open and favorable terms encouraging wider adoption and innovation.

Uber and Facebook offer APIs to open new markets. Most notably, Uber expanded its platform by integrating taxi reservations into hotel booking systems. Facebook used its API to create markets for ads and developments on its own platform. Both networks allow developers to create new applications by providing an API. Airbnb is the opposite. It does not offer APIs or SDKs, even though Airbnb is in the process of making itself more open. The consequence of a missing API is that no interfaces are available to receive, analyze, or validate the data, leading to high information control. It also means missed business opportunities that could be realized by providing official APIs.

The more open a platform, the more new users it can attract and the more development users can do in the channel. APIs and SDKs can enhance technical and content quality. A platform that is envisaged to become an ecosystem needs transparency and documentation. The reason for neither being transparent nor providing platform boundary resources is that any interface bears technical and business risks. Technical risks can involve cyberattacks, data theft, or viruses. Business risks involve any platform user locking in other users and transferring them out of the platform. Another form of business risk is users copying the network's business model.

Access and Control

This element contains several questions for its operationalization. They include:

- Accessibility: does the sponsor make the network accessible to all, or do they impose restrictions? Whereas restrictions and control mechanisms may improve quality and increase transparency, they also come at the expense of the quantity of applications and services provided and potential user growth.
  Facebook started with restrictions. Only people affiliated with a university were allowed to sign up. In 2006, this restriction was

removed, prompting massive growth for the platforms. WeChat requires verification to open business accounts, increasing barriers to entry but promising, in return, more safety and transparency about who uses the network.

- Input control and security: once the sponsor decides on the rules for joining the platform, they must be implemented. A platform allowing users to be completely anonymous, like Reddit, only needs minimal checks on new accounts, are needed. They can be fully automated. A network with a claim to exclusivity, like some platforms for venture capitalists, implements much more sophisticated checks. Potential new users need to undergo a *Know your customer* process. Often, a platform's agent will contact the new user, leading a face-to-face discussion with them to inquire about potential investment width and breadth.

- Output control and monitoring: networks operate an output control mechanism to check the transaction conducted over the platform. Think of retweets, stars, and likes as examples. Some platforms like Facebook, Google, or Apple have one side rating the other. Others have all sides rating each other, such as Alibaba, Uber, and Airbnb. Ratings by network users are especially popular because they resonate well, at least with one side of the intermediation, creating trust and reducing costs for the sponsor. Instead of the network's sponsor rating the transactions, the customers do it. In any case, there is a need for a meta-process to handle complaints and problems in the transaction itself.

- Safety: people using networks need several types of safety. They expect the platform to work technically, that is, safeguarding from cyberattacks, data theft, or viruses. However, they also expect the transactions to lead to the intended end. People using Airbnb expect safe and sound accommodation. People using credit cards expect to purchase a product. The sponsors of a network need to make the network deliver on these expectations and have mechanisms in place to react in case of any breach.

- Process control: digital business models rely on processes. Non-digital business models rely on processes, too, but they can be circumvented. In digital networks, the process architecture determines usability and the transaction rates of people using the network.
- Openness: the resulting feature of all these aspects is the network's openness, which will be discussed in more detail below. However, this discussion showed that the decisions about access and control are full of trade-offs. Many platforms take their time to experiment with decisions and how they influence the network's connections and transactions.

The Value of Trust

The technical security of the network is one thing. How users and potential users perceive it is another matter. Many networks use several devices to increase the trust of their users in their network. Some of these devices are ratings, categorizations, transparency, custodianship, or contractual guarantees. More about trust and risk will be discussed below.

Pricing Structure

We already discussed the more technical aspect of pricing in Chapter 3. Viewed from the point of view of governance, the leading pricing decisions to be taken are:

- Does the platform pursue transaction-based pricing or an all-in fee?
- Does the network require registration fees?
- What is the relationship between free and paid content?

4.4 Integration

As we have already outlined, the question of how open a network should be is essential for its governance. In addition to the more technical aspects of openness, as discussed before, there is a more strategic one, referring to a network's relationship to other networks. Does the network aspire to exclusivity, complementarity, or integration?

To understand the problem, let us introduce a new term: vertical integration. This term is familiar among pipeline business models. If, for example, the South Korean company Lotte manages supermarkets, owns the industries that produce these supermarkets, and even owns the primary agricultural production facilities for these commodities, then it is vertically integrated.

Vertical integration refers to corporate consolidation whereby the vertical range of manufacture is increased by merging several companies with successive processing or trading stages. A company possesses various stages of its value chain.

Other forms of integration also exist, such as horizontal and diagonal integration. *Horizontal integration* is used when companies on the same value chain level cooperate or buy each other out. For example, when one bar buys another or two carpenters' shops merge, this is an example of horizontal integration. Diagonal integration is when companies that have nothing to do with each other buy each other out or set up business units. So, if a textile manufacturer acquires a mountain railway or a shipping company establishes a business unit for paper production, these companies undertake diagonal integration.

Vertical integration plays a significant role in network business models, forming the basis for exclusivity claims. For example, when Apple produces hardware and software, it exemplifies vertical integration and an associated claim to exclusivity. In contrast, Microsoft's focus on software makes it more compatible and integrative. The logic of vertical integration is as follows: the more vertically integrated a network, the greater its claim to exclusivity; the more centralized its governance, the more it intervenes in the offerings and decisions of its users; the more uniform its technical specifications, and the more differentiated its pricing, thus maximizing its ability to exploit willingness to pay.

Compatibility and integration refer to how well a network works with others or incorporates them into itself. Intermediary platforms like Tripadvisor are compatible, allowing users to book hotel rooms through multiple channels simultaneously. Tripadvisor is one such channel and does not claim exclusivity. It is linked to other booking platforms. Similarly, hotels post their rooms on various channels, including Tripadvisor.

Integration goes a step further than compatibility. Rather than merely *tolerating* another use or inserting a link, it incorporates the added value of another network into its own. For instance, when booking via Tripadvisor and paying with PayPal, Tripadvisor integrates the PayPal network into its own.

Compatibility also pertains to how someone on one side of the market reaches those on the other. The Visa payment system is compatible in that any bank can participate, but it remains exclusive to nonbanks, especially American Express.

Which one is better, exclusivity or compatibility? This question cannot be answered in general terms. It is always dependent on the network, in concrete terms, on the specific business model. Consider the following pointers:

- Standards claim exclusivity because they only reduce or eliminate transaction costs if all users implement them. This is why the Hypertext Transfer Protocol Secure (HTTPS) on the internet and the metric system, for example, have established themselves as standards.
- Network operators favor exclusivity, believing it locks in customers and shuts out competition. For example, there is no movement toward cross-brand compatibility in the video game market.
- Network operators often support exclusivity because it lowers capital expenditures and operating expenses. For instance, one argument for using Blu-ray was that it would establish a new industry standard, allowing all providers to implement the same low-cost production technology and then focus on competing for content.
- Network sponsors may prefer compatibility and integration if they aim for rapid growth, innovation, and scaling. After a long exclusivity period, Apple moved toward compatibility upon

realizing its offerings lacked diversity. Airbnb is also moving toward compatibility and integration because it believes it has lost innovation and needs external influences.

- Many networks rely on compatibility and integration to quickly achieve critical mass, providing low-threshold access and facilitating scaling.

- If standards are allowed to differ, they may coexist success-fully. Apple and Microsoft's operating systems have survived by specializing in different markets: Microsoft concentrated on homes and businesses, while Apple specialized in graphics and education. Magazines represent another example of platforms differing in many dimensions and coexisting.

- Networks that are too exclusive can experience leakage. If the governance established by the network's sponsor makes the network unattractive, users will bypass it and approach each other directly. This disintermediation occurs primarily when networks are too vertically integrated, demand excessively high prices, are too complicated to operate, are too exclusive, or are simply boring.

- Users can circumvent exclusivity claims by using multiple networks with exclusivity claims, such as Google and Duck-DuckGo, side by side. Technically, they can also develop their programs to bypass exclusivity. The Tor browser, for example, is based on Firefox, but users integrated it into Tor.

- Empirical studies by Parker and Van Alstyne (2018) indicate that the more open ecosystems are—focusing on compatibility and integration—the more successful they are commercially and economically. Commercial success means higher profits, while economic success means increasing the welfare or benefit of all participants. Parker and Van Alstyne describe this as "permis-sionless integration," leading to "permissionless innovation." *Permissionless* implies free access. They emphasize that the less protected the intellectual property of the network operator is, the more innovations are generated by users, leading to greater network effects and spill-over effects—innovation transferring to others.

How Open Should a Platform Be?

Open networks operate on multiple sides, are not vertically integrated, are compatible with others, and even strive to integrate others. Closed networks provide a clear and conclusive definition of the market sides, aspire to exclusivity, and rely on uniform, centralized governance and vertical integration.

The benefits of being open include diversity, innovation, access, scaling, and commercial and economic welfare effects.

The benefits of being closed include control, integrity, quality assurance, less complexity, and security.

Despite this broad discussion, the consensus is that network operators ought to retain at least ownership of the subroutines that make the network work. Meta rules are also supposed to come from the operator, even if the meta rule is that there are no rules.

4.5 Trust and Risk

Networks are communities of trust. The more people using the network trust each other, the more permanent connections the network can establish, and the more transactions will develop. Therefore, a critical governance task for the network operator is establishing a trust-building mechanism that provides security in connection quality and minimizes risks.

This is not straightforward. The difficulties arise from the very definition of trust. Trust has a different meaning in different contexts of life. Regarding the network economy, the term can never refer to a moral value or an ethical standpoint. It refers to a person's ability to use and rely on the network. Mayer et al. (1995) define trust along these lines:

Trust: The willingness of a person to be vulnerable to the actions of another person based on the expectation that the other will perform a particular action important to the trustor, irrespective of the ability to monitor or control that other party.

This definition encapsulates two things: First, trust is about depending on the other person to do what they promise. And second, there are no major control options. It is precisely these features of the network that lie at the heart of its governance. How can network operators establish trust in this functional sense? They use signaling and sanctioning, which we will review later. Let us first see some defining aspects of trust:

Trust is a mechanism for coordinating action in networks:

- It reduces transaction costs by reducing complexity and creating access.
- It breaks down uncertainties about the actions of others by being based on identification, shared purpose, and mutual benefit.
- It connects the present to the future by making it clear that an established connection will endure and that the connection's success and failure will remain in the collective memory of the network.
- It facilitates the faster exchange of information. People who trust each other are more willing to share information. A lot of information is also already in the collective memory of the network.
- It facilitates conflict resolution, on the one hand, as it emphasizes voice rather than exit. Voice implies that the people in conflict are incentivized to exchange ideas and resolve the conflict. Exit, however, involves dissolving the relationship and leaving the conflict unresolved.
- It leaves scope for non-perfect but pragmatic solutions to problems.

Trust can be understood in several ways, although their application to network business models isn't always straightforward. First, there is trust based on norms, which refers to shared and socialized values.

People have learned to set aside pure self-interest in favor of the greater good by adhering to norms that promote this value. Shared norms generate solidarity and provide resources for bonding and bridging different interests. However, applying this type of trust to networks, mainly commercial ones, can be challenging.

Second, trust acts as a mechanism for reducing complexity. In a complex world, social exchanges must be managed to simplify interactions. Trust allows people to behave under the assumption that their expectations of others' actions will be met. This assumption is based on generalizing experiences that eventually become routine, leading people to believe that things will work well. Many networks leverage this reduction in complexity to build trust, though this type alone is insufficient, as it is vulnerable to disappointment.

Third, there is utilitarian trust, which develops when people pursue a common goal. Even if they have no reason to depend on each other, pursuing a shared goal that benefits everyone can foster trust. Many networks exploit this form of trust. However, it is important to note that the reason for collaboration and trust may disappear once the common goal is achieved.

Lastly, there is trust as social capital. Social capital describes the level of social cohesion within communities, encompassing processes that create networks, establish standards, and build social trust to facilitate coordination and cooperation. This term applies specifically to groups, but each individual must build their stock of social capital to enable collective potential. Attributes such as reliability, quality of work, strength of character, and reputation contribute to this stock. The more these attributes are confirmed through interactions with others, the larger the stock becomes. This is the critical aspect of trust for platform business models. Consequentially, networks seek to implement this mechanism through signaling and sanctioning, which are easy ways of reinforcement learning to create and maintain a stock of capital.

Trust in networks develops gradually and is more process-oriented than person-oriented. Offers and experiences are collected, and efforts are made to gather as much information as possible. This requires both information (signals) and institutional reminders (sanctions). Initially, the decision to trust is often utilitarian, aiming to achieve a common goal. Over time, as more positive experiences are gained, the type of trust evolves within the network, becoming a means of reducing complexity for participants who assume that everything will work out well. When people strongly identify with the network, social capital forms in at least some individuals, which then expands to the entire community and, eventually, the network system as a whole.

Two levels can be distinguished here:

1. Instruments designed to build trust, based on information transparency and securing institutional reminders within the network, facilitate and accelerate this development.
2. Institutions that promote trust in networks include mechanisms that increase the frequency and openness of communication, duplicate relationships, build an institutional record of connections and their outcomes, balance autonomy and dependency, make the reputation of individual participants clear and transparent, and ensure transparency in the selection and integration of new partners.

Greater trust and effective trust-building mechanisms minimize risks, though they can never eliminate them. Every interaction carries some risk, but it can be reduced to a manageable level for participants. It is important to distinguish between two modes of risk impact: the network and the individual users.

4.6 Signaling and Sanctioning

As mentioned above, signaling and sanctioning are effective instruments for building trust as social capital because they rely on reinforcement learning. They include everyone in the network, keeping the platform's collective memory alive. Most network business models employ them, so we should get a grasp of them.

Anyone searching for accommodation on Airbnb sees information about the apartment and the person renting it out. Typically, this includes details about the host, such as their location, how long they have been on Airbnb, whether they are a Superhost, the number and nature of their reviews, and whether they have been verified. If verified, the specific information checked for accuracy, such as identification card (ID), selfie, email address, and telephone number, is clearly stated.

This information helps other users of the platform assess the reputation of a potential business partner. Although it does not predict how the partner will behave in a specific situation, it provides insights into who you are dealing with. This information indicates whether you can trust this partner or whether caution is advised. This concept is fundamental to signaling theory, defined in economic theory as follows:

Signaling is part of information economics and addresses problems in principal–agent theory. The agent has more information about a situation than the principal and sends signals to reduce uncertainty and persuade the principal to enter into a contract.

Information economics, which analyzes economic systems considering incomplete information, forms the basis of the signaling approach. It acknowledges that perfect information does not exist, often putting one person at an informational disadvantage. Consequently, the less informed person must invest additional resources to overcome this information deficit, which is costly and complicated and may lead to network leakage, as with all governance problems.

Economist Michael Spence tackled this issue in the early 1970s and developed the signaling concept. This approach mitigates information deficits by obliging the better-informed party to disclose information through signals. These signals describe various activities or characteristics that may ultimately change the expectations of the transaction's subject.

Signaling theory originated in the labor market, describing the signals that future employers receive from job candidates. It is essential to distinguish between four types of signals, though only the last three effectively bridge the information gap between potential contractual partners:

- Conventional signals: these are general statements and assertions that can be interesting but are easy to make without truthfulness. They can be seen as small talk or dismissed as cheap talk.

- Index signals: these evaluations, such as letters of recommendation or assessment evaluations, are conducted by independent third parties.
- Handicap Signal I: related to the present, these signals are more expensive to send for low-quality offerings than for high-quality ones, such as a good CV or diplomas with high grades.
- Handicap Signal II: related to the future, these signals make low-quality actions expensive for the individual, such as a willingness to forgo a position if a pending examination is not passed.

In economic theory, *handicap* refers to signals related to qualitatively inadequate actions. Qualitative here means whether a person meets specific characteristics, such as completing an economics degree or working on a Six Sigma project.

These four elements can be transferred to networks. For instance, various networks rely on these signals in their relationships. Newspapers facilitate comments, Amazon actively encourages customer feedback, and Tripadvisor's primary process is based on customer reviews. This brings us back to the example at the beginning: Airbnb.

Example: Signaling in Airbnb

Information about the apartment, description: Conventional signal

Indication of the place of residence of the potential landlord: Index signal

Indication of how long the person has been with Airbnb: Index signal

Superhost: Handicap Signal I

Reviews: Handicap Signal I

Verification: Handicap Signal I

> Handicap Signal II would be a satisfaction or money-back
> guarantee or promise that the apartment is remarkably
> inexpensive, flexible, equipped, and so on, for use.

The use of signals and, consequently, the accumulation of social capital in the form of reputation pay off. Empirical studies have revealed that there is a price gap on Airbnb. The more often a host is rated, the lower their price. This is true for all hosts. It is still unknown why this price gap exists. However, the lower the host is rated, the more the price for their accommodation decreases with increasing ratings. If we look at hosts rated in the top 20 percent of all hosts, the price drops by 27 cents per rating. Those in the second quintile see their price fall by 54 cents per rating. And for hosts around the median, the price drops by 81 cents per rating (Teubner et al. 2017).

Signaling alone does not lead to trust. Trust is a consequence of functioning connections, which primarily means that the connections and exchange processes must work. While trust may simplify and accelerate them, it is not a sufficient condition for a network to function.

Many network operators are eager to make the connection or interaction process as simple and secure as possible. They often provide their payment processing solutions or manage them entirely. They often organize shipping and similar processes and ensure that the progress of exchange relationships is transparent for everyone involved in the exchange.

Yet networks also intervene if a person breaks the rules, makes transactions impossible, disrupts connections, gains money at the expense of others or the network, and generally breaches the signals they have sent out. When networks sanction people who use them, this is called sanctioning.

In this context, sanctioning is a form of play of the signaling theory. This is because it involves making the shortcomings of the person's actions public and anchoring them in institutionalized reminders. If Uber lets people who drive and those who are driven rate each other, the rating remains *forever*. If Maria is given one star by the driver Sonja, this star remains in Maria's account and drags her star average down. Ricardo, an online auction platform, displays all auction entries. Each person has a list with positive, neutral, and negative ratings that can be accessed anytime.

Sanctioning makes transgressions public and consequently reduces a person's social capital or reputation. The rationale behind this is that if the network implements sanctioning quickly and effectively enough, it reduces the social capital of this person yet increases social capital overall because it is rewarded with trust by the members for good governance. It goes without saying that if a person repeatedly breaks the rules, they must be removed from the network.

4.7 Transferring Reputation

Sanctioning and signaling are person-related measures. They reinforce or diminish the social capital of the user. Many people are users of several networks at the same time. Many people join networks on a recommendation by another person who is already a member. This brings a new set of questions: If social capital is reputation, how can it be transferred, if at all? More systematically:

- *Intra-network reputation*: is it possible to transfer one person's reputation within a network, at least partially, to another person in the same network?
- *Inter-network reputation*: is it possible to transfer a person's reputation from one network to another, at least in part, for the same person?

The answer to the first aspect is yes. In many networks, one person's reputation can be transferred to another. Letters of recommendation in the labor market fulfill precisely this function. In many private clubs, prospective members must be recommended by existing members. At least initially, Airbnb required recommendations from existing members with a good reputation before accepting a new member for accommodation rental.

However, it is important to note that only part of the reputation is transferred; not all social capital required for acceptance is passed on. The individuals must provide or build up the remaining part through signaling. Reputation remains person-oriented. By the way, the transfer of reputation from one person to another in a network is never complete and seldom severed. The sanctions incurred by the network's new members will often affect the recommender's reputation.

The second question is more challenging. Intuition suggests that social capital is closely linked to the person holding it, making it seemingly straightforward for the same individual to transfer their capital from one network to another. However, empirical findings show that social capital cannot be easily transferred between networks.

For example, Paul drives for Uber and has a five-star rating. If the rating were only and exclusively personal, it would be conceivable that Paul could transfer his five Uber stars to his Airbnb rating if he started renting out accommodation. But this is not currently the case. Personal reputation cannot be transferred from one network to another—even if it is the same person. Several possible explanations come to mind:

- Uniqueness of networks: each network may be perceived as unique and incomparable. Reputation in one network constitutes a bundle of personal qualities that cannot be applied equally in another. This is questionable since platforms like Uber, Lyft, and Juno use similar bundles of personal qualities, yet reputation transfer between these platforms is impossible.
- Organizer resistance: network organizers may not allow the transfer of reputation, which could conflict with exclusivity claims. This is also not plausible. If reputation is personal, people will find a way of making their reputation in one network known in the other. Additionally, the wish of a network to have it nontransferable does not follow that it is nontransferable.
- Technical feasibility: even in ecosystems where integration is essential, and the entire system would benefit from such a transfer, it may not occur because the technical possibility of implementing it has not yet been found. This seems implausi-

ble, too. Most reputation systems are easy to understand, which
makes them, in principle, easy to transfer.

- Independent attempts: the repeated attempts to make reputation
transfer technically feasible speak against the lack of technical
solutions. Independent clearing houses for reputation, such as
TrustCloud, Briefly & Whytrusted, connect.me, TrustRank, and
Legit, have all attempted this. Most have disappeared from
the market, with TrustRank existing under a different business
model and Deemly and Traity offering *reputation passports* in
niche markets at best.

- Economic theory: reputation depends on the reputable person
and the people trusting them. Social capital consists of individual
and community capital, making it only partially transferable and
challenging to transfer. Social capital, or, as it can also be called,
reputation, is situation-dependent, contingent on the network in
which it has flourished and is deployed. This explains why it is
easier to transfer within a network than across networks.

These approaches, some complementary and some conflicting, do
not imply that inter-network reputation transfer is impossible. The
potential benefits of such a transfer would be enormous, prompting
ongoing attempts to implement it. These explanations highlight the
problems, but it will be the task of entrepreneurial individuals to solve
them.

A promising approach views reputation as a function involving
two variables: the person (or personal qualities) and the situation (or
situational qualities) within a network. When these two variables, or
the bundles of qualities they represent, can be transferred, building
inter-network reputation or capital is possible.

4.8 Strength of Networks

Networks exhibiting good governance are strong. Yet, how do you
model their strength? This depends on the perspective from which this
strength is assessed. One point of view is the economic or business one.

The other is the science of putting networks together, cybernetics. Let us review both.

The Economic Perspective

Profit is an economic measure indicating whether income exceeds expenditure. If this is the case, people reward the company with a profit. However, if expenditure is higher than income, users show the company the yellow card, signaling the need to change its business model to offer added value. If the company cannot do this, it is eliminated from the market, akin to receiving a red card. Profit is only a benchmark for network business models once critical mass has been reached.

Capitalization refers to a company's capital, consisting of equity and borrowed capital. Having sufficient capitalization is always crucial for networks, especially at the beginning, before critical mass is achieved. Capitalization finances the network business model until it can generate capital independently, that is, until it becomes profitable.

User numbers are a vital indicator of network development. The absolute number of users is important, but so are the rate of change and the distance to critical mass.

Additional economic and commercial figures include the number of transactions conducted via the network, the turnover of information within the network, the number of resolved conflicts, the development of APIs, and the welfare of the people using the network.

A network can also be measured on its capacity to respond to disruptions. In this case, we differentiate:

- Robustness: a network's ability to function and mediate expected connections or transactions despite external disruptions. For example, if the supply chain for industrial components is disrupted, an online business-to-business platform that can still mediate the components demonstrates robustness by connecting companies that would not usually be considered procurement sources.

- Resilience: a network's capacity to recover quickly after an initial disruption, compensating for or replacing any loss of members and connections. For instance, if a disruption causes members of a business-to-business platform to leave, the network can quickly recruit new members by pivoting to industries that have not previously exchanged on the platform.

The Cybernetic Perspective

In addition to business and economic metrics, technical measures are developed explicitly for networks. Cybernetics, the science of networks, evaluates the strength of networks, distinguishing between the following elements:

- The network map: the network needs to be mapped in an operationalized form.
- Key nodes: identifying key and central nodes of a network.
- Connection strength: assessing the strengths and weaknesses of connections within and within the network.
- Cohesion: measuring how the network interacts.

Network theory uses the concept of centrality to identify key nodes, referring to individual members with a particularly high number of connections to others. When two central members have direct connections, a key node is formed. Direct connections between members with numerous connections result in strong network effects, while breaks in these connections negatively impact the entire network. Connection strength and network cohesion can be determined using the following dimensions:

- Betweenness: the likelihood that a person using the network will follow the most direct connection route and become involved in other people's connections.

- Closeness: how quickly a person can reach others in the network and how quickly they can be reached.
- Eigenvector: how well a person is connected with well-connected people or pivotal figures.

With this, we have come full circle. To launch a platform, we need a business model. After much tweaking the model, we need measures for our success. These measures must be of an economic or business nature. But we also need to keep an eye on the technical side. Networks are primarily technical constructions. They will not yield an economic benefit if they do not work technically.

4.9 Governance Strategies

These different aspects of the network business model, its connections, pricing, and governance, were already outlined in an article published in the *Harvard Business Review* in 2006 (!) by Thomas Eisenmann, Geoffrey Parker, and Marshall W. Van Alstyne. They sketched out what is still the common take on platforms and networks today. A summary of their article also serves as the main takeaway of this book:

Two-sided markets, or platforms, connect two distinct user groups that interact through the platform. Prominent examples include credit cards that connect consumers and merchants and video game consoles that link players and developers. The authors identify three main strategic challenges for managing platforms: pricing the platform, coping with winner-take-all competition, and dealing with the threat of envelopment.

Pricing the Platform

Pricing is a crucial aspect of two-sided markets because platforms must set prices for both sides of the market. The challenge is determining which side to subsidize and which to charge a premium. This decision hinges on understanding cross-side network effects, where the platform's value to one group depends on the size of the other group.

Key Considerations

- Subsidy side versus money side: typically, the side of the market that is more price-sensitive or essential for attracting the other side is subsidized. For example, Adobe offers its Portable Document Format (PDF) reader for free to users (subsidy side) to attract a large user base, making the platform valuable to document creators who pay for the software (money side). This approach ensures a broad base of users, increasing the platform's attractiveness to paying customers.

- Quality sensitivity: platforms might need to subsidize the side more sensitive to quality to ensure high standards. For instance, in the video game industry, platforms like PlayStation or Xbox often subsidize consumers to ensure a large user base. This strategy attracts high-quality developers who are assured of a market for their games, ensuring that the platform offers compelling content.

- Output costs: pricing decisions are more straightforward when each new subsidy-side user costs the platform provider essentially nothing, as with digital goods like software. However, platform providers must be more cautious when a giveaway product has appreciable unit costs, such as tangible goods. If a strong willingness to pay does not materialize on the money side, a giveaway strategy with high variable costs can quickly lead to significant losses.

- User sensitivity to price: generally, it makes sense to subsidize the network's more price-sensitive side and charge the side that increases its demand more strongly in response to the other side's growth. Adobe's Acrobat software follows this pricing rule, making its reader software free to attract users while charging writers who value this large audience.

- User sensitivity to quality: high sensitivity to quality also marks the side to subsidize. This pricing prescription can be counterintuitive: rather than charge the side that strongly demands quality, you charge the side that must supply quality. This is evident in the video game industry, where platform providers ensure high-quality standards by imposing strict licensing terms and charging developers high royalty.

Coping With Winner-Take-All Competition

Due to network effects, many two-sided markets are prone to winner-take-all dynamics, where a single platform can dominate the market. This competition is intense because the platform's value increases with its user base, creating a self-reinforcing cycle.

Strategies to Address Winner-Take-All Dynamics

- Determine market conditions: assess whether the market will support a single platform or multiple platforms. For instance, the digital video disc (DVD) market was likely to be dominated by a single format due to high multi-homing costs for consumers and studios and limited opportunities for differentiation. Understanding these conditions helps businesses predict whether the market will consolidate around one platform.
- Sharing versus proprietary control: companies must decide whether to collaborate on a shared platform or compete for proprietary control. Shared platforms can expand the total market and reduce competitive expenditures. For example, creating the DVD standard involved industry participants cooperating to avoid a costly standards war similar to the VHS–Betamax conflict.
- Winning the battle: a company needs cost or differentiation advantages to fight successfully. Three critical assets include preexisting relationships with prospective users, a reputation for past prowess, and deep financial resources. First-mover advantages can be significant, but they are not always decisive. Late movers might avoid the pioneer's positioning errors, incorporate the latest technology, or reverse engineer the pioneer's products to beat them on cost.
- First-mover versus late-mover advantages: first-mover advantages are crucial in platform battles but are not always decisive.

Late-mover advantages might be more significant in slow-evolving markets, as seen with Google in the web search industry. Google avoided the clutter of early portals, focusing on a simple, fast-loading homepage, and improving on overture's paid-listing model.

Dealing With the Threat of Envelopment

Envelopment occurs when a platform provider in an adjacent market enters the market, leveraging overlapping user bases and offering a bundled solution that incorporates the original platform's functionality. This strategy can threaten standalone platforms by making their offerings less attractive.

Counter-Envelopment Strategies

- Change business models: adapt the business model to mitigate the threat. When it launched its Rhapsody music service, RealNetworks shifted from subsidizing consumers to charging them directly, moving from a streaming media to a subscription service model.
- Form alliances: small platforms can partner with larger companies to enhance offerings and fend off envelopment. RealNetworks partnered with cable and phone companies to bundle its services, increasing its value proposition. These alliances can help the smaller platform providers offer a more competitive package against the enveloping threats.
- Legal remedies: companies can use legal strategies to challenge anti-competitive practices. RealNetworks successfully sued Microsoft for antitrust violations, securing a significant settlement. Legal action can provide a crucial lifeline for smaller platforms facing envelopment by larger rivals.

Platforms' success in two-sided markets hinges on strategic pricing, effective competition management, and the ability to counteract envelopment threats. Companies that master these strategies can achieve sustainable growth and dominate their markets, leveraging the unique advantages of two-sided network effects.

4.10. Critical Assessment

While Chapters 2 and 3 deal with the usual characteristics of networks, network effects, and pricing, this chapter focuses on governance. Network effects and pricing constitute necessary criteria for a network's functioning. Yet only the *right* governance is sufficient. Like many authors cited in this chapter, we can go one step further and say that networks are governance systems.

Moreover, pricing can also be treated as a function of governance, as this chapter suggests. With this in mind, network effects would result from governance decisions made by the network operator.

While the discussion surrounding network effects and pricing can be carried out on a technical level, the discussion about governance is both technical and practical. It can also be conducted both qualitatively and quantitatively. Given that the previous chapters focused on a strong analytical and quantitative strand, this chapter primarily presents governance qualitatively.

The most important lesson from governance strategies is that governance is trial and error. No one can say in advance how open or closed, how much signaling and sanctioning, or indeed which pricing strategies will work. Practical experience with networks commonly regarded as successful suggests that governance is always in transition. Depending on the network development phase, a different package of governance instruments is required. It is likely that the governance of a network also depends on the market's maturity as a whole. So, the more people are active in networks, the more diverse the packages of governance measures within a specific network will be.

We can generally reach the following conclusion about the network economy: it is always in flux. The way we deal with it—whether theoretically or practically—is a learning process in itself. Economic models associated with the network economy seem to be lagging behind reality. Despite this, these models serve as a guide, help to understand how the network economy functions, and provide resources for the further development of analog and digital platforms.

Lastly, some overarching reflections on the network economy will be elaborated:

- Looking back: the network economy is not a new concept. Networks have always been an integral part of economic processes. Whether it is common assets such as communal land or early industrialization, they were all networks. Networks seem to be especially well suited to involving people in economic processes and producing and distributing welfare. In the same token, networks appear to give particular preference to the operators or organizers of the network when welfare is distributed. Economically (and presumably also normatively), this is not a problem. It can, however, generate controversy.

- Looking forward: thanks to the emergence of powerful microprocessors, cloud technology, the omnipresence of the internet, increased bandwidths, and more diverse and high-performance programming languages, it is likely that the network economy, especially digital platforms and ecosystems, will become even more widespread. With this in mind, we can expect it to initially rival pipeline business models and overtake them. Yet, it will not be able to replace pipelines. This is because the people working in networks may be small, but they are pipeline business models. It is even conceivable that small pipeline companies have better cards in the network economy when compared to large companies and groups designed as pipelines.

- Looking inward: research into network economics is only beginning, not least in business administration and economics. They are only asymptotically approaching the reality of networks, as presented in the various chapters of this book. Their models still lack completeness and are ponderous. They can only be implemented with imprecision through trial and error. The research desiderata are correspondingly predetermined: More work will need to be undertaken in the context of governance

concerning openness and building trust. This will also give
rise to pricing models. This approach will presumably make
it possible to better model network effects. A parallel strand
of research addresses the importance of data management for
digital platforms. What data consists of, who it belongs to,
how it should be safeguarded, and how it can be transformed
into revenue streams for people and network operators are all
relevant questions. Another field of research deals with measuring networks' strength, robustness, and resilience. All these
research fields will never achieve a final verdict because economic
theory involves systematically dealing with problems emerging
over time and with innovation. Given that time and innovation
progress, theory is subject to a constantly renewing learning
curve.

- Looking outwards: networks are not alone. Just like the entire
economy, they belong to and interact with society. This means
they are also bound up with questions of political desirability,
ethical notions, openness to innovation, and structural change.
Even if networks, particularly digital platforms, generate and
distribute welfare, certain groups in society might be skeptical
of such economic structures. It is, therefore, quite conceivable
that resistance to the proliferation of networks will arise. Uber
has been banned several times in Germany; the European Union
has considered regulating large network operators as *gatekeepers*.
These endeavors are not economically tenable, yet the political
logic is not based on economic theory. In the same way that
networks resisted and acted against the advent of industrialized
pipeline business models—they wanted to defend their sinecures
or, as they are known in economic terms, pensions—it is
conceivable that pipelines will continue to exert political pressure
on networks today and in the future. However, politics usually
plays no role in the long term since the economically superior
solution comes out on top anyway. This is not without its
consequences, however. If digital platforms catch on, the people
who work with them will require new skills. People operating

platforms will also require new sets of skills. And the structural and technical infrastructure will also need to be adapted.

Economic theory cannot make any normative recommendations, irrespective of where the outlook is directed. It can study, model, and, most importantly, understand economic phenomena. The only normative advice is that given in "A Hitchhiker's Guide Through the Galaxy"—which reads:

"Don't panic."

Summary

- Governance refers to a system of rules and processes for controlling a network to ensure connections are created and remain sustainable.
- The objective of governance in networks is to implement network effects for the benefit of all participants.
- Governance is the main component of the service architecture in network business models.
- Elements of network governance include governance structure, resources and documentation, access and control, trust and risk, pricing, and external relationships.
- Concerning monitoring, the decision regarding exclusivity, complementarity, or integration is fundamental.
- Equally fundamental is whether the network is open, that is, allowing as many people as possible to take part, or closed, that is, following a more centralized, regulated governance.
- Trust is the foundation for connections and exchange relationships in many networks. The network operator's task is to set up instruments to safeguard trust.
- Signaling can be used to establish and safeguard trust. This involves assigning various pieces of information about a person's trustworthiness in the network, such as feedback, satisfaction, and background checks.
- Signaling is a way of building and safeguarding trust. It involves assigning certain information about a person's trustworthiness

in the network, such as feedback, satisfaction, and background checks.

- Sanctioning is also used to build trust. It secures the institutional reminder of people or connections that have not fulfilled the network's governance.
- Networks are robust in their governance if they can absorb or even resolve disruptions that originate outside of them.
- Each network business model requires its own strategy, including concerning governance. General recommendations may be applicable but never resolve the business decision.

Review Questions

First Series: Which Statements Are Correct? Which Are Not?

1. Governance refers to the rules for managing a company.
2. Governance is a hygiene factor, particularly in networks.
3. Governance in networks allows network effects to unfold.
4. Access and control arise from the specific business model; therefore, they are irrelevant to decision-making.
5. Open networks tend to grow faster than controlled networks.
6. Open networks are generally more innovative than controlled networks.
7. Open networks generally exhibit higher quality than controlled networks.
8. Signaling is a mechanism by which information is made public.
9. Signaling is a mechanism for establishing and maintaining trust.
10. Sanctioning is the exclusion of a person from a network.

Second Series: Solve the Following Challenges

1. Which governance functions does the bouncer of a disco fulfill?
2. Compare the access control of two dating platforms, Parship and OkCupid.
3. Compare the governance structures of Facebook, WeChat, Alibaba, Airbnb, Uber, Google, and Apple.

4. Compare the resources and documentation of Facebook, WeChat, Alibaba, Airbnb, Uber, Google, and Apple.
5. Compare the access and control (control, input, output) of Facebook, WeChat, Alibaba, Airbnb, Uber, Google, and Apple.
6. Compare the trust instruments of Facebook, WeChat, Alibaba, Airbnb, Uber, Google, and Apple.
7. Compare the external relationships of Facebook, WeChat, Alibaba, Airbnb, Uber, Google, and Apple.
8. Compare the pricing of Facebook, WeChat, Alibaba, Airbnb, Uber, Google, and Apple.
9. Provide an example of a robust network.
10. Provide an example of a resilient network.

Third Series: Respond to the Following Questions and Solve the Mini-Case Studies

1. Why is pricing an element of governance here when it was considered an independent economic instrument in Chapter 3?
2. What does it mean exactly when the claim is made here that governance represents the actual service architecture of the network?
3. To what extent are the governance strategies presented in Section 5.9 still topical? The article cited was, after all, published in 2006.
4. To what extent do the governance strategies presented in Section 5.9 need updating? Undertake this task.
5. What does the statement "The product of the network involves the reduction of transaction costs" mean, and how is it related to the governance of networks?
6. How do signaling and sanctioning function in pipeline business models? Provide two examples of each and compare them with the networks.
7. What would be the advantages and disadvantages of inter-network reputation transfer on the level of entire networks?

8. What would be the advantages and disadvantages of the inter-network reputation transfer on the level of individual people using networks?
9. Devise approaches and implementations for transferring reputation in intra- and inter-networks.
10. How does the envelopment of networks function? Provide two examples.

Questions

Commented Bibliography

- Eisenmann, Thomas, Geoffrey Parker, and Marshall van Alstyne. "Strategies for Two-Sided Markets." *Harvard Business Review* 84, no. 10 (2006): 92–108.
  - o This Classic Article on Strategy, Generally, and Network Governance.
- Mayer, Roger, James Davis, and David Schoorman. "An Integrative Model of Organizational Trust." *The Academy of Management Review* 20, no. 3 (1995): 709–734.
  - o This Article Discusses Trust Extensively from an Economic Perspective. It Covers the Elements of Trust and Certain Operationalizations.
- Moon, Francis. *Social Networks in the History of Innovation and Invention* (Springer Netherlands, 2014).
  - o This Book Integrates the History of Science and Technology with Modern Social Network Theory. Using Examples from the History of Machines and Case Studies from Wireless, Radio, and Chaos Theory, the Author Challenges the Genius Invention Model. Network Analysis Concepts Are Presented to Demonstrate the Societal Nature of Invention in Areas Such as Steam Power, Internal Combustion Engines, Early Aviation, Air Conditioning, and More.
- Parker, Geoffrey and Marshall Van Alstyne. "Innovation, Openness, and Platform Control." *Management Science* 64, no. 7 (2018): 3015–3032.

- o   Precise and Empirically Guided Examination of the
     Consequences Arising from the Openness of Networks. The
     Article Implies That Openness Has More Welfare Effects
     than Control and Closeness.
- Teubner, Tim, Florian Hawlitschek, and David Dann. "Price
  Determinants on Airbnb: How Reputation Pays off in the
  Sharing Economy." *Journal of Self-Governance and Management
  Economics* 5, no. 4 (2017): 53–80.
  - o   An empirical study on the monetary value of reputation,
       taking Airbnb as an example, is needed.

Glossary

Benefit: The perceived improvement in an individual's or entity's situation resulting from a particular action or interaction. Benefits drive people to join or engage in networks to enhance their well-being.

Business Model: A strategic plan outlining how a company will create, deliver, and capture value. It includes target customers, value propositions, revenue streams, and service architecture, guiding the company in achieving its business objectives and managing risks.

Capital Expenditure (CAPEX): Funds a company uses to acquire, upgrade, and maintain physical assets such as property, industrial buildings, or equipment. CAPEX aims to increase the company's operational capacity, enhance its productive efficiency, and boost sales and profits.

Chicken and Egg Problem: A challenge in network business models where a network needs a critical mass of participants to be valuable, but it also needs initial participation to attract more users and reach that critical mass.

Critical Mass: The minimum number of participants required in a network for network effects to become significant, enabling the network to provide value to its users.

Crowding-Out Effect: A situation where excessive participation in a network reduces the overall and individual benefits, potentially diminishing the network's value.

Discovery Process: An economic process characterized by an undetermined outcome involving numerous interactions, reactions, and counter-reactions. Less regulation and more decentralization generally benefit the participants by fostering spontaneous and beneficial outcomes.

Dynamic Pricing is a strategy in which prices are adjusted in real time based on demand, supply, and other external factors. This method helps businesses maximize revenue by setting prices according to individual or situational circumstances.

Ecosystem: A digitally connected network of multiple interaction structures, supporting various subnetworks and fostering synergistic relationships among participants.

Elasticity: Specifically, price elasticity of demand, which measures how sensitive the quantity demanded is to a change in price. High elasticity indicates significant changes in demand when prices change, while low elasticity indicates little change.

Governance: A framework of rules and processes to control and manage a network. Governance aims to facilitate sustainable connections and optimize the network effects for all participants, forming a crucial part of the service architecture in network business models.

Investment: The allocation of money, time, or resources to an endeavor expected to yield future benefits, such as cost savings, increased efficiency, or revenue growth.

Model: A simplified representation of a complex reality used to explain and predict relationships between variables. Models are used to formulate hypotheses and test their validity.

Network: A system of interconnected individuals or entities that interact and depend on each other, facilitating the exchange of information, goods, or services.

Network Business Model: A business model that targets multiple complementary groups, creating value by facilitating interactions and leveraging network effects.

Network Economy: An economic system that utilizes the structure of interconnected interactions among individuals or entities to achieve economic goals and enhance value.

Network Effect: The phenomenon where the value of a network increases as more participants join. Conversely, the value decreases if the network loses participants.

Operational Expenditure (OPEX): Recurring expenses necessary for the day-to-day functioning of a business, such as rent, utilities, and salaries.

Pipeline Business Model: A traditional business model where value is created through a linear process, with each step adding value sequentially.

Platform: A digital network managed by an entity that develops or commissions the core infrastructure, enabling interactions between user groups.

Price Differentiation: The strategy of adjusting prices based on different customer segments, situations, or market conditions to maximize revenue.

Pricing/Price Setting: Determining the monetary value assigned to a product or service, often based on cost, demand, competition, and perceived value.

Reputation is the overall perception of a person or organization, reflecting trustworthiness and reliability. In economic terms, reputation is part of social capital and influences how others engage with the entity.

Sanctioning: Actions taken by a network's governance system to penalize participants who violate rules or norms, such as raising prices, issuing warnings, or expelling them from the network.

Signaling: A concept in information economics where one party (the agent) sends signals to another party (the principal) to reduce uncertainty and encourage contractual agreements. This addresses the information asymmetry in principal–agent relationships.

Subsidization: The practice of lowering prices for one group within a two-sided network using revenue from another group. This can enhance value creation by leveraging indirect network effects.

Transaction Costs: The expenses incurred in conducting a business transaction, including costs for transferring goods, gathering and assessing information, and considering alternative options.

Trust: The willingness of one party to rely on the actions of another, based on the expectation that the other will act in the trustor's interest, even without the ability to observe or control their actions.

Value Creation: The process of generating more value than the cost of inputs, measured as the difference between sales revenue and the total production costs.

References

Atlantic Telephone and Telegraph Company. 1908. "Yearly Report." AT&T.

Belleflamme, P., and M. Peitz. 2018. *The Economics of Platforms.* Cambridge University Press.

Choudary, S.P., G.G. Parker, and M. van Alstyne. 2015. *Platform Scale: How an Emerging Business Model Helps Startups Build Large Empires With Minimum Investment.* Platform Thinking Labs.

De Reuver, M., C. Sørensen, and R.C. Basole. 2018. "The Digital Platform: A Research Agenda." *Journal of Information Technology* 33(2): 124–135.

Eisenmann, T., G. Parker, and M.W. van Alstyne. 2006. "Strategies for Two-Sided Markets." *Harvard Business Review* 84(10): 92.

Forbes. 2021. "World's Largest Corporations." *Forbes Magazine* 32: 35–39.

Gassmann, O., K. Frankenberger, and M. Choudury. 2020. *The Business Model Navigator: 55 Models That Will Revolutionise Your Business.* Pearson Education Limited.

Knieps, G. 2016. *Network Economics.* Springer Verlag.

Manne, G.A., and J.D. Wright. 2011. "Google and the Limits of Antitrust: The Case Against the Antitrust Case Against Google." *Harvard Journal of Law and Public Policy* 34: 171.

Mansell, R., and W.E. Steinmueller. 2020. *Advanced Introduction to Platform Economics.* Edward Elgar Publishing.

Mayer, R.C., J.H. Davis, and F.D. Schoorman. 1995. "An Integrative Model of Organizational Trust." *Academy of Management Review* 20(3): 709–734.

Mokyr, J. 2018. The Past and the Future of Innovation: Some Lessons From Economic History. *Explorations in Economic History* 69: 13–26.

Munger, M.C. 2018. *Tomorrow 3.0: Transaction Costs and the Sharing Economy.* Cambridge University Press.

Øverby, H., and J. Audestad. 2021. *Introduction to Digital Economics: Foundations, Business Models and Case Studies.* Springer Verlag.

Parker, G., and M. van Alstyne. 2018. "Innovation, Openness, and Platform Control." *Management Science* 64(7): 30153032.

Rysman, M. 2009. "The Economics of Two-Sided Markets." *Journal of Economic Perspectives* 23(3): 125–143.

Schneider, H. 2017. *Creative Destruction and the Sharing Economy: Uber as Disruptive Innovation.* Edward Elgar Publishing.

Schreieck, M., M. Wiesche, and H. Krcmar. 2018. "Multi-Layer Governance in Platform Ecosystems of Established Companies." *Academy of Management Proceedings* 2018(1).

Shapiro, C., and H.R. Varian. 1998. *Information Rules: A Strategic Guide to the Network Economy.* Harvard Business Press.

Somm, M. 2021. *Warum die Schweiz reich geworden ist.* Stämpfli Verlag.

Summit Health Advisors. "2024 State of Healthcare Platforms Report (Summit 2024).": 13–15.

Teubner, T., F. Hawlitschek, and D. Dann. 2017. "Price Determinants on Airbnb: How Reputation Pays Off in the Sharing Economy." *Journal of Self-Governance and Management Economics* 5(4): 53–80.

About the Author

Henrique Schneider is an economist with extensive experience in finance, climate, networked industries, and economic policy. He has served as a regulator and expert on many high-level nonexecutive boards in Switzerland and the United Nations system. He has published several monographs on different aspects of economics and several papers on current issues.

Index

OTHER TITLES IN THE ECONOMICS AND PUBLIC POLICY COLLECTION

Jeffrey Edwards, North Carolina A&T State University, Editor

- *Striding With Economic Giants* by David Simpson
- *Explaining Money & Banking* by Byron B. Carson and Robert E. Wright
- *Dismantling the American Dream* by Michael Collins
- *The Future Path of SMEs* by Amr Sukkar
- *Rebooting Local Economies* by Robert H. Pittman, Rhonda Phillips and Amanda Sutt
- *What Economists Should Do* by David Tuerck
- *The Language of Value* by Virginia B. Robertson
- *Transparency in ESG and the Circular Economy* by Cristina Dolan and Diana Barrero Zalles
- *Navigating the Boom/Bust Cycle* by Murray Sabrin
- *Developing Sustainable Energy Projects in Emerging Markets* by Francis Ugboma
- *Understanding the Indian Economy from the Post-Reforms of 1991, Volume III* by Shrawan Kumar Singh
- *Understanding Economic Equilibrium* by Mike Shaw, Thomas J. Cunningham and Rosemary Cunningham
- *Macroeconomics, Third Edition* by David G. Tuerck
- *Negotiation Booster* by Kasia Jagodzinska

Concise and Applied Business Books

The Collection listed above is one of 30 business subject collections that Business Expert Press has grown to make BEP a premiere publisher of print and digital books. Our concise and applied books are for...

- Professionals and Practitioners
- Faculty who adopt our books for courses
- Librarians who know that BEP's Digital Libraries are a unique way to offer students ebooks to download, not restricted with any digital rights management
- Executive Training Course Leaders
- Business Seminar Organizers

Business Expert Press books are for anyone who needs to dig deeper on business ideas, goals, and solutions to everyday problems. Whether one print book, one ebook, or buying a digital library of 110 ebooks, we remain the affordable and smart way to be business smart. For more information, please visit www.businessexpertpress.com, or contact sales@businessexpertpress.com.

www.ingramcontent.com/pod-product-compliance
Lightning Source LLC
Chambersburg PA
CBHW061309220326
41599CB00026B/4808